THEORY · PRACTICE · ACTIVITIES

AWARENESS & CHANGE

RELATIONSHIP BUILDING BETWEEN CHILDREN, YOUTH AND ADULTS

McPherson Family Life Center, Inc.
McPherson, Kansas

AWARENESS and CHANGE

Relationship Building between Children, Youth and Adults.

Theory, Practice, and Activities.

Bruce E. Kline, Psy. D.
Kneldrith Kline
Miriam Overholt, M.L.S.

For parents and teachers of children, preschool and grades K-12, in the regular classroom.

Also field tested and adapted to the special needs of:

Gifted, Talented and Creative
Learning Disabled
Special Education
Inpatient Mental Health
Outpatient Mental Health
Single-Parent Households
Children of Addiction

Second Edition edited by Andy Lowe.

Illustrations done for First Edition by Joseph Seale
and dedicated here to his memory.

Cover design by Dawn Lauck.

With a Foreword by Allan Barclay, Ph. D., ABPP

McPherson Family Life Center, Inc.
McPherson, Kansas

Awareness and Change is available from:

McPherson Family Life Center, Inc.
224 S. Maple
McPherson, KS 67460, U.S.A.

Acknowledgement is given to Sandi Alexander and a host of Child Development Assistants with The McPherson Family Life Center who contributed many of these activities from their creative and spontaneous work with the children of the Family Life Education Program.

Acknowledgement and thanks is given for permission to reprint materials from:

A 4-H Pamphlet, Wichita Clover Club, a chapter of the Kansas 4-H Club

Peoplemaking by Virginia Satir, copyright 1972, Science and Behavior Books, Inc., Palo Alto, California

Creative Family Activities by Valerie Sloane, copyright 1976, Abingdon Press, Nashville, Tennessee

Awareness by John O. Stevens, copyright 1971, Real People Press, Moab, Utah

First Edition © 1981
Second Edition © 1990

ISBN 0-9625366-2-8

Library of Congress
Catalog Card Number: 89-63790

Table of Contents

FOREWORD

The present work, AWARENESS AND CHANGE, is designed to be a functional and practical approach to the important issues of helping children and adolescents achieve positive self-esteem. This is accomplished through a graded series of supervised educational experiences that aim at the development of personal skills in relationship building, self-awareness and interpersonal skills. The authors have focused on enhancement of human potential in the areas of creativity and effective use of the self in solving problems.

The work is admirably suited to its purposes and provides clear and explicit behaviors to be elicited from both leader-teachers and student-participants. Goals are presented in the form of objectives found in the exercises contained in each chapter. Especial emphasis is placed on fostering the ability of the student-participant to clearly understand the linkages among activities to be engaged in, and the concept to be learned in each particular exercise.

Thus, the student-participant is brought to an awareness of the relationship between behavior, as behavior, and how that behavior can be generalized to a large life context. This big picture approach to psychological meaning is effectively presented in each chapter. Although this may sound abstract, the authors efforts at linkage development are both concrete and practical, and will help the student-participants to a more sensitive awareness of themselves. Participants will learn the target concept directly in each exercise and will also learn to become observers of themselves. This is the first step in learning to understand and think about oneself. The results will enhance the range and versatility of personal response repertoires for both youth and adults.

On balance, this work promises to provide a clear, proven, and well-conceptualized approach to the enhancement of potentialities in young people. This is accomplished in the areas of relationship building and self-awareness, and in relation to the more effective functioning of youth as students, as problem-solvers and decision makers, and finally as human beings.

I commend this book to the reader.

Allan Barclay, Ph.D, ABPP

Associate Dean for Academic Affairs

Wright State University

School of Professional Psychology

Editor of the *Journal of Professional Psychology*, an APA publication.

Consulting Editor for: *Perceptual and Motor Skills*
Psychological Reports
Psychotherapy and Private Practice

AWARENESS and CHANGE:

Relationship Building Between Children, Youth, And Adults

Theory, Practice, And Activities

INTRODUCTION

Many parenting aids are available in books and self help classes today. Some are practical programs of listening and problem solving, some emphasize behavior management, while others focus on identification of feelings, natural and logical consequences, or communication skills. Few programs, however, blend all of these major components of life awareness, behavior, and thoughts and feelings, into a coordinated and organized approach to development. Further, few programs integrate these themes with the vitally important theme of *relationship development* and interpersonal bonding between child and adult.

Self help parenting books and classes often focus on manipulation of the child and parents who have had more than they can bear. Much less research and publication effort has been invested in how to build relationships between adults and their children.

To teach and emphasize behavior manipulation alone may well provide environmental and child controls, but it may foster children who are dependent on direct pay off or external sources of approval. Punishing objectionable behavior can eliminate the unacceptable behavior, but it will also produce fear reactions toward the punisher. To rely primarily on listening and problem solving may facilitate emotional growth and better solution finding, but alone it does not provide adequate growth experiences for children.

Relationship building must be a continuous process and does not happen without effort. This book presents a wide variety of carefully chosen activities and games for parents, teachers, and their children to enhance that process. Specific development and relationship building goals are clearly marked and introduced in each chapter of focus. Above all, the principle purpose of the book is to teach and promote healthy, rewarding relationships between children and adults. It may be easy to find things to do with children. It is quite another thing, however, to locate significant *relationship building activities* that have been laboratory and field tested.

The activities in this book have been created and organized to meet the child's developing functional and personality needs.

Family desire to promote and secure harmony in the household and at school is universally reported. The focused activities and exercises of this book have been researched and tested by parents in the home, by elementary and secondary school teachers, by counselors in schools and family life centers, and by social workers with parents and children for both inpatient and outpatient settings. Psychologists and psychiatrists in private practice and in hospitals with acute chronically ill children have also found the ten chapter curriculum and activities very useful in their efforts to gain rapport and treat children. Art and music therapists have found many of the exercises useful as adjuncts to their specific focus for treatment. Field tests have also documented success with exceptional children ranging from the exceptionally gifted to those with low level functional abilities.

The activity is a vehicle for *relationship building* between adult and each targeted child.

These exercises have also been used successfully with many auxiliary books and philosophies of change. Some notable examples include:

Arent, R., **Stress and Your Child**. Englewood Cliffs, New Jersey: Prentice Hall, Inc., 1984.

Canfield, J. and H. Wells, **100 Ways to Enhance Self-Concept in the Classroom**. Englewood Cliffs, New Jersey: Prentice Hall, Inc., 1976.

Chinn, P., Winn, J., and Walters, R., **Two Way Communication with Parents of Special Children**. St. Louis, Mo.: The C.V. Mosby Co., 1978.

Clark, B., **Growing Up Gifted**. Columbus, Ohio: Charles Merrill, 1979.

Delisle, James R., **Gifted Children Speak Out**. New York: Walker & Co., 1984

Dinkmeyer, D. and G.D. McKay, **Systematic Training for Effective Parenting**. Circle Pines, Minn.: American Guidance Service, Inc. 1976.

Frankl, V., **Man's Searching for Meaning**. New York: Washington Square Press, 1963.

Gallagher, J.J., **Teaching the Gifted Child**. Boston, Mass.: Allyn & Bacon, Inc., 1975

Ginott, H.G., **Between Parent & Child**. New York: MacMillan Co., 1965

Ginott, H.B., **Between Parent & Teenager**. New York: New American Library, 1975.

Hallahan, D.P. and J.M. Kauffman, **Exceptional Children**. Englewood Cliffs, New Jersey: Prentice-Hall, Inc., 1978.

Jourard, S., **Self-Disclosure and Experimental Analysis of the Transparent Self**. Melbourne, Florida: Krieger, 1971.

Jourard, S., **The Transparent Self**.

Kline, B.E., "A Naturalistic Assessment of Whole Family Treatment Effects Based on Systematic Training for Effective Parenting," McPherson, Kansas: Mingenback Family Life Center, 1977.

Kline, K.E., **Taking Charge**. Winona Lake, Indiana, 1983.

Kline, B.E. and E.A. Meckstroth, "Understanding and Encouraging the Exceptionally Gifted", **Roeper Review**, 1985.

Kramer, A., Executive Ed., **Gifted Children, Challenging Their Potential New Perspectives and Alternatives**. New York: Trillium Press, 1981.

Lowe, A., with B.E. Kline and K. Kline, **Strengthening Families: A Practical Approach**. McPherson, Kansas: McPherson Family Life Center Inc., 1985.

Patterson, G.R., **Living with Children**. Champaign, Illinois: Research Press, 1968.

Briggs, D.C., **Your Child's Self-Esteem: The Key to Life**. Doubleday & Company, Inc.: Garden City, New York, 1970.

Vail, P.L., **The World of the Gifted Child**. New York: Walker & Co., 1979.

Webb, J.T. and E.A. Meckstroth, Tollen, S.T., **Guiding the Gifted Child**. Publishing Company: Columbus, Ohio, 1982.

Please see the suggested reading lists at the end of each chapter for other related sources of value.

PREFACE

This book is designed to be a functional and practical tool for parents and teachers. It is a digest of important concepts with accompanied activities, games, and events, coded by chapters to facilitate each of the ten developmental goals. Most of the activities are appropriate for an adult and one or many children. In each case, it is suggested that the adult leaders model the goals and aims suggested in each chapter introduction. As progress is made through the book, the step by step process of a developing relationship between adults and children is fostered through time sharing, goal setting, problem solving and accomplishment, mutual encouragement and others. All of these functional interpersonal skills are encompassed in the tested, coded and enjoyable activities of the book.

Each chapter heading is introduced separately with a concept rationale and explanation of its relevance. Each chapter is also divided via subtitles into several classes of events, such as orientation and introduction, interaction activities, individualized activities, arts and crafts, related books, and posters suitable for photocopying. All of the activities have been selected and field tested to complement the major themes of each chapter.

The first two chapters focus on enhancing *awareness* of body and feelings in self and others and are designed to prepare children and adults for the eventuality of change. It is only through awareness that change can become intentional and therefore purposefully adaptive. For each of us, inviting our children to become active in our lives is an indicator that we are balanced between internal and external controls of influence. We are thus prone to external agents of control whether they be intimidation in the work place of school bullies. Most importantly, self-awareness is a prerequisite for self activated change. Chapter 1 focuses attention on *body-awareness*, and Chapter 2 highlights *awareness of feelings and emotions*.

The third and fourth chapters emphasize different phases of *encouragement*, (positive reinforcement). In Chapter 3, the focus is on *self-reinforcement*, the importance of self-talk, and how what we say to ourselves influences us in whatever we think or do. In Chapter 4, *positive reinforcement* is taught. This is accomplished via selected activities which emphasize encouragement of the people with whom we wish to build a relationship and/or directly influence. Whether it be adult to children or the reverse, data indicates that children access these skills as readily as adults, (Kline, 1977). In the context of relationship building as a model for influence and parenting, encouragement of self and others is very likely the single most potent tool in promoting self-awareness and positive relationships.

It does make a difference how we deliver the messages we send. Chapter 5 highlights the importance of claiming our own messages with a self-reference that is personalized or owned by the speaker. With such *"I" messages* there is no ambiguity in the source of encouragement or criticism. The strong and overt suggestion is that when a claimed message is positive, the receiver know who likes the behavior and approves of the person. When the message is negative, the receiver can identify who is unhappy and disappointed. The receiver may then choose to directly confront, ignore, or assertively negotiate the difference. But when the source of a negative or disapproving statement is ambiguous, such as "we don't do things like that" or "Mommy doesn't like that", the child is often left with a momentary and involuntary need to translate the message before thinking about it or responding. Some children fail to break the code of such ambiguous statements and miss both the meaning and the potential personal potency of the message.

Body language is a fascinating component of communication. Chapter 6 centers on activities that focus child and parent attention toward awareness of body language and sensitivity to these subtle communications from others. The teaching format is activities and games that can be fun, but that also familiarize the participants with a purposeful content.

When emotions cloud our thinking or overwhelm us, the most needed response from those who care about us is to listen to our feelings as well as our verbal content. It is through this identification of emotion and acknowledgment of feelings that we are able to clearly proceed toward problem solving and the necessary steps of resolution. Chapter 7 presents activities and games for small groups or individuals with the context of developing sensitive *listening skills*. It also fosters the importance of gaining the ability to admit, present, and disclose our own feelings openly to a selected and trusted listener.

When listening has diffused the emotional cloud, we often have the need to solve the dilemma that has been bothering us. Chapter 8 presents several different formats to be used in *problem solving*. It also teaches the necessary skills to utilize good problem solving techniques. There is a mini drama with roles for up to ten or more participants and exercises for personal goal setting, brainstorming, and evaluation.

Work skills are learned behaviors that all too often are not attended to. We assume that these skills are learned on the job. This is less and less possible today as the world becomes progressively more complex in function as well as relationships. Many parents and teachers would like to teach their children and young teens the value of work and the skills and values necessary to be effective as adults. They often try to do it, however, by simply giving work tasks or projects and chores to their children. This most often meets resistance. Chapter 9 concentrates on two forms of mutual work activities, *helping and cooperation*. Differences between the two are explained and a variety of games, exercises, and ideas are presented that focus the helping and cooperation skills for children as they are developing. Since these skills also require responsive leadership, parents, and teachers are challenged to practice the acquired skills of encouragement, listening, effective communication, and problem solving as models for youngsters in this context. In observing their models practicing such positive interpersonal skills, youth are strongly reinforced in the acquisition and practice of help and cooperative activities at home and school.

Finally, Chapter 10 presents a variety of fun *warm up activities* for verbal and physical space ice breakers in group and individual settings. These are especially useful for individuals who are not well acquainted in any group setting such as at school, day care, group therapy, Sunday School, etc. Games as fillers while waiting are also described to prevent disorganization when order is needed in an otherwise empty time slot.

Bibliographies of suggested readings are included in the Introduction and after each chapter.

The Appendix presents a list of *LP recording* that are useful and listed to fit the focus of several designated chapters in the manual.

A *feelings word list* is provided to enable practice in naming the feeling experiences for many people.

Puppet construction technique is presented to enhance the creation of valuable resources in role pay and other fun and useful activities.

A list of activity related *recipes* is provided that will ease the use of many cooking and food preparation sections of the book.

In each case, teachers, mental health professionals, and other facilitators for children are strongly encouraged to learn and model interpersonal skills presented in this book. Through this, children are exposed to the rudiments of healthy and productive human interaction. It is our belief that the result of these shared experiences will be *firmly rooted relational skills, strengthened relationships,* and *accessible emotional intimacy* that will sustain the challenge of each child's future.

Finally, it is often assumed that as youngsters progress in their development, all levels of awareness and understanding are equally paced. This is not often the case. For example, it is common for youngsters to lose visualization, fantasy, and inner self-awareness abilities, often as a result of criticism of punishment. As a result they grow into adults who are unaware of (not sensitive to) their own or others feelings, their bodily needs, or their state of emotional being. All of these greatly impact a person's capability to manage stress. Adults are often less flexible than children in choosing or being able to change. Seemingly elementary activities may be very appropriate for any age person, including all adults. If children see adults modeling openness to these activities and the learning of these skills, they can learn the beginning fundamentals of interpersonal growth and social relationships. Their steps into adulthood will thus be less encumbered with low self esteem, insecurity and self doubt.

We spend a large segment of our early life in formal education learning a variety of subjects and functional skills. One of them is not parenting. Only rarely is there instruction in how to gain and maintain healthy, happy relationships. Models for parenting and relationship building are most often those of our own parents. Our parents did the best that they were capable of doing. The high social and emotional demands of our society require exceptional flexibility. It is our hope that the enhanced model of parenting and adult modeling presented here will also encompass the best in relationship building philosophy and activities. This book is dedicated to that end.

Bruce E. Kline

Kneldrith E. Kline

Miriam E. Overholt

CHAPTER INTRODUCTION

Awareness is a prerequisite for purposeful change. We can change only those things in ourselves of which we are aware. Looking at ourselves may not be easy or pleasant, but it is the first step toward positive personal change and is also the first order of business in *relationship building*. Self-awareness is therefore the first order of business in this book. It is a process, not an event. As the process occurs, new doors of acceptance open and new potentials for life are seen. We may each begin to realize that our unique characteristics are acceptable. We are not strange because we are different from other people, nor do our similarities mean we are common or unimportant. As we grow in self-acceptance, we gradually leave behind the fears that bind us to old self defeating behaviors. Positive change thus becomes possible. When this process is initiated with children, they can begin a life of positive adjustment and flexibility with maximum ease.

Some of the basic assumptions, believed and implemented by the authors of this book, are that children are people, their values and feelings are important, and they can make life affecting changes when given the opportunities and encouragement no matter what their age. Since learning by doing is an effective and enjoyable teaching method, the ideas explained in each chapter of this book are designed to be explored, understood, and practiced through the activities which follow them.

INCLUSIVE LANGUAGE

In order to use inclusive language and to avoid the awkwardness of he/she, her/him, the gender has been alternated from chapter to chapter. For example, Chapter 1 uses all masculine pronouns; Chapter 2 uses all feminine pronouns, and so on. An attempt has been made to use both female and male gender in a variety of activities in order to avoid traditional sex role stereotyping.

It is our belief that both boys and girls should be given the opportunity to participate in activities designed to develop skills and attributes, such as assertiveness, warmth and empathy, that will prepare them to function effectively as well-rounded human beings and members of society.

HOW TO USE THIS BOOK

Each chapter begins with two explanations of the learning objectives. The first is directed to the leader, and the second is directed to the participants.

The chapter objective introduction is explained first of all to the leader of the group. This explanation is designed to familiarize the leader with the general ideas of the unit. Further reading is available for each chapter and is strongly recommended to each leader. Some suggested references are listed at the end of each chapter.

The chapter objective introduction for participants follows the leader introduction for each chapter. In this section there are suggestions for what the leader is to say to the participants. Each time an activity is used from the chapter we strongly recommend that the leader read or paraphrase the related printed segments. This is because the purpose behind each activity is thus reinforced repeatedly for the participants. They will begin to make a *direct connection* between what they are doing in the fun activity and the learning process. *This awareness is essential if the participants are to fully benefit from the concepts and use them elsewhere in their lives!* These introductions are not mutually exclusive, and both may be useful to leaders and participants alike.

Awareness of Body and Awareness of Feelings are the first two concepts presented. The next seven chapters deal with the tools for change. Self-Reinforcement as Stress Management and Positive Reinforcement (Chapters 3 and 4) are methods of encouraging myself and others toward success. "I" Messages (Chapter 5) help me take responsibility for my statements and present them to others without judgment. An understanding of Body Language (Chapter 6) can increase the strength with which my messages are communicated. Reflective (Active) Listening (Chapter 7) is a tool to help others express emotion and to group consensus in decision making or as a solution to a problem, and Helping and Cooperation (Chapter 9) are skills for investing in people and tasks around me. Chapter 10 offers fun games and exercises which will encourage your group to relax and feel comfortable together.

The book is designed for use with primary, preteen, and teenage children. Most activities can be used with minor modifications for more than one type of learning experience or age level. We encourage you to modify freely to fit your situation and needs. Remember, however, that *your primary task* as leader *is to help the youth understand the link between* what they are *doing and the concept* being associated with that doing. This program offers family life education to each member of participating families from adults to toddlers. *Awareness and Change* may be used with children's programs in many settings from preschool toddlers through high school and beyond.

Finally, our field tests strongly support the fact that adults who use these materials will find themselves positively influenced though learning communication, listening and awareness strategies, and other components of this book. (Kline, B.E., 77)

Best wishes on your adventure into the pleasures of *Awareness and Change*.

CHAPTER 1

Awareness Of Body

INTRODUCTION OF CONCEPT

Body awareness is having a picture of what I look like, how I sound and smell, and how I feel when touched or touching. This includes knowing my body and how it works.

As I become more aware of my body, I realize that there are parts of me which I like more than other parts. By knowing the way I am and by accepting rather than rejecting myself, I can come to respect and like myself more fully. This process opens the door for me to change unhealthy attitudes about myself and others into healthy awareness.

Body awareness is learning to listen to my body. My brain receives messages from the different parts of my body which tell me that I am warm or cold, my arms are tired, my back is aching, my stomach is full, or any other message. I may have learned to disregard some messages from my body. For example, if someone told me to "be quiet" every time I talked about a certain hurt, I might grow to ignore the feeling that I am hurting although the pain is still there. Or, if I received caring attention only when I was hurting, I may have been taught to create hurt in order to receive the attention I needed. Body awareness involves learning to listen to all parts of myself again, so I can hear messages I had been ignoring. I can also learn to eliminate the false hurting messages as I learn to receive the attention I need as a result of positive existence and positive achievement.

Body awareness is essential to a strong sense of self. Children are often not respected as being full human beings and as a result can lose physical self-respect and contact with their bodies. Young teens in particular are often very vulnerable to extreme feelings of self-rejection and over awareness of their bodies. This is often focused on potential development and devaluing or strongly overvaluing their sense of self through targeted body parts. Providing the suggested activities may help them get reacquainted with their bodies and sense of self and will encourage them to learn about their uniqueness from the inside. In addition to this, they will learn to appreciate the opinions of others. This internal basis of orientation is essential to self-acceptance. It also sets the stage for a stronger internal focus of control and a resulting reduced susceptibility to external influences. This is very important for youth as they establish their personal self-worth and values. Will they look primarily to others for decision, or into their own wisdom, psyche, and heritage? This and the following concepts may enable youth to group the best of their environment using a sense of self.

INTRODUCTION TO PARTICIPANTS

Our bodies are like the houses in which we live. Each is special and different from every other, although we are more alike than different. It can be fun for us to explore our bodies and find out how we look, sound, smell, and feel. Our senses are the doorways into our houses.

Name The Senses And
Discuss The Function Of Each

THE MAIN SENSES:

Sight . . . . . .what we see
Auditory . . . .what we hear
Smell . . . . .odors we smell
Touch . . . . .things we feel
Taste . . . . . .things we taste

Other Senses That We Use To Gather Information
About Our World:

Barometric . sensitivity to atmospheric pressure
Balance . . . how we keep upright (in equilibrium)
Temperature how we sense hot and cold
Pain . . . . . how we feel hurt
Vestibular . . how we stay in balance
Eidetic . . . how we see mental images
in our mind's eye
Geomagnetic how we sense magnetic properties
of the earth

Ionic . . . . . our awareness of chemical processes
Infrared   . . . our sense of invisible rays beyond
                          red in the spectrum
Infrasonic . . our sense of sound beyond
                          usual audible range

When we look into a mirror, we see the picture (reflection) of our bodies. When we listen to ourselves talk or sing, we hear sounds which are made in our bodies. When we hold an arm or hand close to our nose, we smell that special scent which is ours alone. When we touch something (even the soles of our feet on the floor), we feel that touch against the outer covering of our bodies which is our "skin". As we learn about our senses, we will get better acquainted with our bodies and know better how to live in them.

We can change some things about our body houses, but other things will remain the same as they are. We can exercise to develop muscles, eat more or less to become bigger or smaller, have braces on our teeth to straighten them, and curl our hair or leave it straight. But we do not have much control over making ourselves taller or shorter, and we cannot change the basic colors of our skin.

What other things do you think of that cannot be changed? What other things do you think of that can be changed?

(DISCUSS)

As we grow older, there will be some changes in our body houses which will take place without our doing anything to make them happen. What are some of these?

(ALLOW TIME TO DISCUSS)

We are going to do some things which will help us get better acquainted with our body houses. Each house is important and valuable; each is excellent and good in its own way. Our bodies are different shapes, colors and sizes, and they are all useful. We can learn to respect and enjoy them. We can teach them to be more useful, beautiful, and enjoyable places to live.

Questions For Discussion:

1. What color is your body house? What other colors have you noticed? Have you ever seen a spotted house (freckles)?

2. As our bodies grow, what changes happen? (Deal

with puberty if appropriate.)

3. When body houses get older, what changes do you notice in them (hair, skin, etc.)?

4. Do you like living in your body house? How would you like it to be different?

5. What things can you do to change your body house, to help you like it more?

6. Can you lean to help others like their houses? How?

7. What can we do when our body houses do not do what we want?

8. Notice as many differences between your body house and your friend's as you can.

9. Notice as many similarities between your body house and your friend's as you can.

INTERACTION ACTIVITIES

T.V. Interview "Name That Person"

Appoint one participant to be a TV interviewer, another is the interviewee. The interviewee has a particular person in the group in mind whom he describes to the interviewer. When the interviewer recognizes and picks out the participant being described, the roles change; interviewee becomes interviewer, "recognized person" becomes interviewee (describer). As various persons in the group describe and hear descriptions, they recognize differences and increase consciousness of personal characteristics. Ground rule: only *positive* or "neutral" descriptive statements are acceptable. Variation: Interviewee (describer) uses only claimed "I" messages (e.g. "I believe she has brown eyes").

"Someone I Know"

The leader begins by giving clues and stating a distinguishing *positive* characteristic of someone in the group. Expand on positive description giving the group opportunities to guess who is being described from time to time. When group members begin to "click in" to how to play the game, invite them to "describers", always utilizing positive characteristics for the descriptions.

Identification Game

Materials: three or more blindfolds

Let three or more participants sit or stand blindfolded in front of the group or within the circle. Invite another group member to describe one of the three in positive statements. The blindfolded persons are then to identify themselves from the descriptions as they are given by group members. Emphasize positive characteristics. Use personality characteristics as well as physical ones. The purpose of the activity is to help participants become aware of themselves as unique, valuable individuals.

Name That Food

Prepare a plate of tray with small pieces of various foods such as raw fruit, vegetables and cheese. Ask the group to name each food and talk about where it comes from.

Blindfold participants and have them taste each food. See if they can name what they are eating. How does taste change when eyes are closed? Ask them to hold their noses closed as they eat to observe how taste changes without smell. Can they name the food by tasting it with both eyes and nose closed?

Smelling Game

Objects to be used for the Smelling Game should have definite odors. Examples are onions, various spices, coffee, soap, perfume, flowers, and paint. Blindfold participants and have them name the item that is held in front of them by identifying the smell. Discuss with the group various odors that occur in ordinary situations, such as cooking, a newly mowed lawn, etc. A journal of smells could be kept with illustrations.

Guided Imagery (Movies In Your Mind)

Have participants take a comfortable, separate position and *close their eyes*. Instruct them to imagine that they are in a beautiful place which is familiar to them and where they would like to be. Continue as follows speaking slowly: "Look around you very carefully. You are in your own special place. Notice the sights around you. Notice the feel of what is underfoot, the smells, the sounds, the time of year. Is it spring? winter? summer? See the colors and forms your mind creates. What do you recognize? As you walk along, look for a friendly person or an animal. When you see it, make a friendly approach and ask if there is something special for you to see or hear. If so, listen and look. Take time to make sure you understand (pause), then thank your friend and start back to where you came from. Look and listen as you move back noticing what is around you. When you are ready, open your eyes and be here." Allow each person time to describe his experience. If the group is more than 5-7, divide for sharing. Encourage positive reflections. Active listen to any negative reactions.

Sight Experiences

Provide a variety of sight experiences such as pictures of beauty in nature, people fighting, breathtaking buildings, sick people, abstract design, war scenes, and people hugging. Use many different colors, patterns, designs, and shapes. Ask the group members to share feelings they associate with each of the pictures.

Walk A Perfect Line

Draw a straight line across the room and give the first person a pair of binoculars. Invite him to look through the large lens at the line. It will appear small and distorted. He must keep his heel and toe on the line as he walks and looks through the binoculars. This is much harder than it seems, and it may help persons realize their dependence on visual perceptions.[1]

Taped Sounds

Divide into small groups and give each a tape recorder and blank tape (the number of groups can be based on how many tape recorders are available). Separate the groups so they do not readily hear each other. Instruct each group to brainstorm sounds they can make and to tape them. Encourage them to be very creative with their resources. Give each group a chance to play back their tape for the whole group and to discuss the sounds.

Sound Experiences

Provide many different sound experiences (see Sound Effects record) for the group. Ask persons to name the sounds and tell what words come to mind to describe each one. Ask if they have feelings associated with any of the sounds, where they have heard these sounds before, which sounds they like the least, the best, etc.

Now instruct them to close their eyes and name the different sounds they can hear in the room. With eyes still closed, tell them that you will touch a person, and he is to talk for the group. The rest of the group will try to guess who is speaking. Think of other sound experiences for your group.

Identifying Objects And Textures

Fill a paper sack with objects that are familiar. Objects such as a spoon, pen, paper clip, rubber band, comb, penny, spool of thread are good to use. Give each person a turn to shut his eyes, reach into the sack and feel one object. The person names the object (without looking) and describes it.

Variation: Place two pieces each of a variety of textures in the sack such as metal, wood, rock, sandpaper, and various kinds of cloth. Ask persons to find the two textures which are the same with eyes closed. Discuss the differences between rough, smooth, hard, soft, thick, thin, etc. See the next activity "Tough Sensations" for possible questions.

Touch Sensations

Provide each participant with a blindfold and invite each to tie it on so that sight is not possible. Pass an object around the circle for each to touch and feel without comment. Then ask questions, inviting all to participate in response.

Possible questions:

1. When you held the object, what were your thoughts?

2. When you held the object, what were your feelings?

3. When and where have you touched an object like this before?

4. Do things feel different to you when you cannot see them?

5. Does being blindfolded make you more sensitive to touch?

Possible objects to pass around: leaf, sponge, rock, wood, fabric, pencil, use your imagination!

Variation: Use feet instead of hands for the touching sensation. Allow time for each person to describe his sensations and impressions. Be accepting and affirming of all persons.

A "Sensible" Thing To Do

Invite each participant in the group to select a corn chip or similar object which can be experienced by more than one of the senses. Ask a variety of questions to stimulate their sensual perceptions of the object.

Possible questions:

1. Look at your corn chip—tell what you see.

2. Touch your chip—describe how it feels.

3. Smell the chip. Does it have a special aroma? Describe it.

4. Crumble or break the chip. Does it have a sound? Please describe it.

5. Taste the chip and chew it. How does it taste? Can you also hear it? Please describe.

Invite each participant to share his perceptual experiences with positive strokes from others. The exercise will expand sense-awareness, and can build group dynamics.

An Exercise In "Good Sense"

Separate the participants into four groups each of which will be named for one of the senses: The See-ers, The Hearers, The Touchers, and The Smellers. Take a tour during which the various groups experience what takes place by concentrating on their assigned sensory input. Share experiences afterward to expand sensory awareness.

Variation: Actually limit sensory experience during the tour to the one sense assigned or chosen by each group (blindfolds to limit sight, earplugs to limit hearing, hands in pockets for all but the Touchers group). Discuss the perceptions of various persons reinforcing all recognitions, acceptances of each other's ideas, similarities and differences as appropriate. Encourage sharing.

What Is Beautiful

List each of the five senses and ask persons to either write down or verbally name three or four beautiful things they have experienced with each sense.

Examples: Vision—a sunset
Hearing—a favorite song
Touch—a rose petal
Smell—lilacs blooming
Taste—peppermint ice cream

Have members take turns describing their experiences to the group in such a way that everyone can relive or imagine the sensation. Support all results and stress the acceptance of individual differences in taste and aesthetics.

"Finding Out"

Each participant is invited to select a nature object either from a collection for that person, or during a brief "finding" period (e.g. rock, shell, leaf). Each person then describes his object to the group telling whatever he can see, smell, feel, or hear from it. He may also comment as to whether it may ever have been alive, had a special use, etc. The exercise is designed to amplify awareness of one's surroundings including commonplace objects. It may also increase awareness of the senses in examining the object.

Fruit

Materials: one apple, banana, orange, or lemon for each participant. All participants to have the same kind of fruit.

Seat participants on the floor in a circle. Give a piece of fruit to each one (same kind). Explain that each apple, banana, orange or lemon has its own distinguishing features. Ask each participant to "get acquainted" with his piece of fruit and to sense with eyes open and later closed the specific shape, texture and distinguishing characteristics of his fruit.

Then use as many of the following procedures as is appropriate for the group:

1. Divide into pairs. Each person introduces his fruit to his partner and then partners exchange fruit, sensing differences.

2. Combine pairs into medium groups (4-6) and invite participants to make a pile of their fruit in the middle, then each to find his own with eyes closed.

3. Form a circle of all participants. Collect all fruit and redistribute by passing all fruit to the right. Each person is to identify his own and place it in his lap continuing until all have their own fruit. Do step #3 with eyes closed if participants are willing.

4. Process the experience. Allow each person to share.

This activity sharpens senses and directs attention to similarities as well as differences in organic objects.

Sculptor

Have group members pair up and stand facing each other without talking. Ask the taller person in each pair to be the sculptor, and the shorter person to be the clay. Instruct the sculptor to take some time to look at his  partner and become aware of him. Ask the sculptor to notice how the partner holds his body, and to gently move his partner's head, arms, or legs to exaggerate what he sees in his body. If the partner tilts his head back, the sculptor can tilt it back even further, etc. Encourage the sculptor to use his hands as if he were molding clay or wax. The person who is being molded can be aware of how it feels to be changed and moved around. The sculptor will continue to mold the statute until he is satisfied with the result. Ask the sculptors to then step back and examine their work to see what it expresses.

Sculptors must now face their statutes and make their own bodies into an exact copy of the statute. Both persons can then get the feel of the statute and what it expresses. They may switch places and repeat the process. Be sure to allow time for discussion when the activity is completed and to let each person share.[2]

Physical Activities

Ask group members to get comfortable and separate themselves. Now lead them in an exercise such as this: "Focus your attention on your body and your physical sensations. Wherever you notice some movement, tension, or discomfort, express this as an activity such as pushing, tensing, holding. If you are tensing your shoulder, tense it more, and be aware of which muscles you use and how you feel as you do this. Take responsibility for this muscular activity and its consequences. For instance, say to yourself 'I am tensing tightly, and stiffening myself'. Muscular tension is self-produced, so much physical discomfort is a result of this. Take some time now to become more aware of your physical activities, and take responsibilities for what you are doing to yourself."

Debrief by asking persons to discuss how they felt about the activity and what they learned about their bodies.[3]

Unfolding

Ask a participant to fold himself into a tight "package". Invite him to choose another member to "unfold" him. He may cooperate or resist.

Process the exercise by allowing time for spectators as well as participants to share.

Variation: pair off in dyads and do the same exercise.

ARTS AND CRAFTS

Hand Design

Materials: Construction Paper
                   Crayons

Have each person place his hand on a piece of construction paper and trace it. Repeat in different directions five more times. Using crayons or markers, instruct each one to color in the closed spaces. Encourage comments from each participant.

Variation: Try using feet instead of hands!

Body-Busters

Materials: Butcher paper
                   Crayons or markers
                   Scissors

Pair off the group and have partners trace around each others' bodies on butcher paper. Color with crayons or markers or paints to resemble clothing or use pieces of cloth to "dress" the person. Head, torsos, and legs can be cut apart (each body into 3 pieces) and mixed up to see how the group would look if they traded figures.

Make A Picture Portrait

Place separate pieces of paper with each participant's name on one in a container. Each draws a name and constructs a simple, positive picture of the individual whose name he drew using descriptive words (make a limit of 10-12 words, e.g. male, happy-go-lucky, etc.). Use only positive descriptive terms.

On the opposite side of the sheet, draw a simple picture portrait of the individual.

Have the group attempt to identify the person from the descriptive words. If unsuccessful, let the drawing be displayed.

Discuss unique positive characteristics of each person.

Mask Making

Materials: Paper plates
Tongue depressors
(or something like them)
Paints or crayons
Yarn

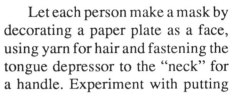

Let each person make a mask by decorating a paper plate as a face, using yarn for hair and fastening the tongue depressor to the "neck" for a handle. Experiment with putting different emotions on the mask faces and having skits with the masks.

+ + + +

Thumb Fun

Materials: Ink pad
Paper
Fine marker

Have each person press his thumb on an ink pad, then print with it on white paper. Discover what kinds of animals and people can be created by adding a few more lines to the prints. Use fine-line markers to add this detail. Encourage comments and curiosity regarding the individuality of the finger prints.[4]

+ + + +

"This Is Me"

Materials: Newsprint or other large paper
Magic markers or crayons
Paste or glue
Scissors
Magazines or
other sources of pictures

Invite each person to make a "This is Me" collage. Have each person lie down full length on the paper. Draw around him to secure shape. Then invite him to choose pictures showing his favorite people, colors, sports, places, foods, etc. and paste them onto his body shape. Allow time for each person to share about his collage. This project may be kept for later modification. New pictures can cover old ones.

+ + + +

Fun With Feet

Materials: Paint (bright colors of tempera)
Large juice cans
Paint brushes
Newsprint or butcher paper
Large sheet of plastic
Low pan of warm, soapy water
Towels
Two chairs

Spread the sheet of plastic on the floor and place a large piece of newsprint or butcher paper on top of the plastic. Put a chair at each end of the newsprint with cans of paint and brushes at one end and a pan of soapy water and towels at the other.

Instruct participants to remove shoes and socks, sit on a chair and paint the bottoms of their feet with colors they select. Invite them to walk on the paper in straight curving lines, leaving their footprints. At the end of the paper, have them step into a pan of soapy water to clean their feet.

Use the same piece of paper for everyone and let each person autograph one of the prints. Hang the finished product and title it by group consensus.

Variations: Prepare a similar mural using hand prints or let persons have their own section of the mural and decorate it freeform with their feet.

Folded People

Materials: Butcher paper or newsprint
              Markers
              (work better than crayons)

Fold three long sheets of butcher paper into three sections each. Divide the participants into three groups, and give each group one piece of the folded paper. Have each group draw a head in the top section, then switch with another group and draw a body under the head, then switch again and draw feet. Before each switch, fold under the sections already drawn on so the next group must guess how to complete the picture. Some interesting characters an be created from this activity. Allow time for group discussion. Guide discussion toward acceptance of differences.

People Pots

Materials: Potters clay or dough
              Paint or markers
              Shellac

Have persons use a rolling pin to flatten clay to about one-half thick and cut out two circles of clay. One circle is the base of the pot and the other is the lid. Give persons a small ball of clay and ask each to roll out about four "snakes" (coils) of clay. Attach coils one at a time to one circle of clay forming a coil pot. Form the lid by attaching a small ball of clay to the other circle. Pinch and pull it to create a face.  Paint the clay and have it fired in a kiln, if possible. Apply clear shellac after firing for a shiny finish.

Variation: Use dough instead of clay following the recipe in the Appendix. Then bake the pots at 350 degrees for an hour. Allow time to cool. Then color with markers and spray with clear shellac. Discuss the differences of the various creations and parallel them to participants uniquenesses. Guide the discussion toward acceptance and awareness of self and others.

Fruit And Vegetable People

Materials: Fruits and vegetables
              Pins or toothpicks

To make life like figures from fruits and vegetables, encourage the group to look at the materials and try to imagine an animal or person. Some examples are: centipede from a long narrow green cucumber with cauliflower floret feet, clown with an eggplant for the body, cauliflower floret for a ruffle, onion for a head, carrot end for a hat, red pepper for mouth, cloves for ears, or radishes for buttons.

Allow time for participants to comment. Encourage persons to be creative and accepting of each other's creations. Use a large variety of fruits and vegetables and have fun. Participants may enjoy contributing materials for this exercise.

Hairy Harry

Materials: Tape
              Tin cans
              Scissors
              Grass seed
              Crayons or markers
              Dirt and gravel
              Construction paper

Invite participants to draw facial features (ears, mouth, eyes, etc.) on construction paper and tape it around the can. Plant grass in the can. It will come up in a couple weeks to provide thick green hair for the person pictured on the can.

Variation: While making the tin can creatures let persons center on one body characteristic and exaggerate it for fun. They can then name their creatures an appropriate name such as "Lippy Lucy", "Nosy Nancy", or "Eyes Edward".

Seed Planting

Materials: Seeds
Soil
Containers for planting seeds

Provide the materials for persons to plant seeds. Watch them grow from week to week. Varieties which sprout rapidly are radishes, corn, watermelon, pumpkins, and beans. Other good growers are tomatoes, carrot tops, and sweet potatoes sections (in water). Nature's growth is an important model for personal growth. Discuss with acceptance and encouragement.

Peanut Growers

Materials: Raw peanuts
Yarn bits (about 2 inches long)
Small paper cups
Pots (4 inches deep,
12 inches across)

Let each person place 1 peanut and 1 bit of yarn in a small paper cup. Every day, moisten the nut and the yarn. (Never cover with water, just make sure peanut and yarn are dampened each day.) The peanut when it sprouts will wind around each yard. When the plant grows to 4 inches it is time to plant in a pot. Keep the pot in a warm and sunny spot. Relate it to body growth and the beauty of all life.

Crystal Gardens

Materials: Glass or aluminum flat pie dish
Wood, cork, sponge, charcoal
or broken pottery
4 T. noniodized table salt
4 T. water
1 T. ammonia

To make an attractive indoor crystal garden, let persons arrange the small pieces of wood, cork, or sponge in a pie dish. Make a solution by combining all the ingredients and pour the solution over the material in the pie dish. Place in a warm room and crystals will grow. Seeing growth can be an exciting and important experience. Relate in a positive way to body growth and change.

Variation: Dip a glass or jar into a mixture of epsom salts and water. The crystals which dry on the glass will not grow, but will stay on the glass if sprayed with shellac.[5]

Sand Painting

Secure plain sand from natural source or lumberyard. Use dry or liquid tempera color paints mixed with a small amount of water to color portions of the sand providing a variety of separate hues.

Fill large salt shakers (or home-made equivalent) with separate colors.

Place glue on paper or other desired surface (e.g. cardboard, wood); shake colored sand onto wet glue sections (shake excess off onto newspaper). Glue may be patterned and when various colors of sand are applied, lovely designs and effects can be secured. Save extra sand and re-use.

Variation: Participants can write their names on the surface with glue, then sprinkle with colored sand. When dry, shake off the excess sand. Cotton, glitter, cereals, corn meal, pebbles, and similar materials may be used. Encourage participants to make colorful pictures of body shapes, parts, names or initials to raise self-awareness.

Sawdust Clay

Materials: 6 cups sawdust
                   (see your local cabinet maker)
                  5½ cups flour
                  2 T. salt

To make sawdust clay, gradually add small amounts of boiling water to the ingredients listed above. Blend thoroughly to form a thick dough (the dough will keep for a week if wrapped in damp cloth or baggies). Encourage persons to play with the sawdust clay and feel the grainy course texture. Instead of stressing production, let each individual leave his own experience with the clay.

✛ ✛ ✛ ✛

You Can Make Your Own Playdough

Prepare playdough (see recipe in Appendix). Use rock or kosher salt if you desire a grainy texture. Let each participant measure and enjoy feeling the ingredients during the preparation time. Give each participant his own piece to form into his own, individual body presentation.

Variation: Any part of the body may be modeled (e.g. hand, foot, etc.).

✛ ✛ ✛ ✛

Feeling Fingers

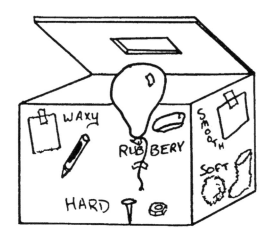

Cover a large box with paper. Cut out words which describe sensations and glue them on the box with touchable examples of each. Some suggestions are:

Smooth —fabric, paper, plastic
Hard—marbles, checkers, lifesavers
Waxy—waxed paper

Rubbery—flat rubber sponge,
    rubber bands
Rough—sandpaper

Invite participants to work with preparation of the box if they are of appropriate age and development. Ask them to bring assorted materials to put in the box. Cut an opening in the top and let them reach into it. They can feel each object and describe it for the group. The box may be put in a learning center where they can use it individually.[6]

✛ ✛ ✛ ✛

Touch-Me Person

On a large sheet of paper, draw a face and let the group add materials to make hair, clothes, cap, eyes, ears, mouth, nose, or beard. Use materials that have definite textures such as:

Hard—wood shells
Soft—fur, yarn
Smooth—metal, plastic
Rough—sandpaper, bark
Crisp—paper, cellophane
Prickly—pine cones, cactus
Spongy—foam, sponge
Springy—coil
Scratchy—styrofoam, wool
Silky—feather, silk

Encourage participation and creativity in choosing and assembling the various materials. As they complete the picture, discuss the different materials used for facial features. Which were fun to touch, and which did persons avoid? Which seemed the most similar, and which the most different? Provide time for persons to share about the experience.

Variation: This can be an individual activity if enough supplies are provided.[7]

✛ ✛ ✛ ✛

"You Find It" Mosaic Designs And Pictures

Materials: Plywood, cardboard or equivalent

Seeds or similar "you find it" materials of any kind, e.g. white or red beans, rice, corn, wheat, barley, caraway, etc.

Shallow container for each kind of seed

White glue

Participants discuss and plan pictures related to their bodies and/or its parts (simple designs are most effective). Participants then draw their individual designs on the plywood or cardboard. When designs are prepared, have them apply a thin coat of white glue to an area of the design and fill the area with seeds or desired material. Apply glue and seeds to each area until the picture is complete, a "mosaic or natural color and texture". Discuss how the body and/or its parts are "living potential" like the seeds.

Paper Binoculars And Telescope

Materials: Paper towel and toilet tissue tubes

Tape

Give each person two toilet tissue tubes taped together for binoculars or a paper towel tube for a telescope and let him decorate it. He can look through his device out a door or window or across the room. Have him describe what he sees to the group. Encourage and accept all efforts; work for group acceptance of all.

Blind Clay Sculptures

Give each person a hand-sized piece of clay. Ask him to close his eyes and form the clay into an image of whatever he desires. Discuss how the absence of sigh affects the creation.

A Closer Look

Materials: Magnifying glass

Variety of objects for viewing—objects from nature such as rock or a blade of grass, and manufactured objects such as newsprint or a coin

Let each person use the magnifying glass to look at some of the objects. Have him describe what each object looks like and how it looks different under the magnifying glass. This activity can be done outside with objects found in nature.

Blind Drawings

Provide paper and pencils for each participant. Invite them to look at an object (the hand they don't write with will work well) and to draw it without taking their eyes off the object or lifting pencils. Encourage them to draw the contour of the object and to try and get a feel for its shape. "Primitive" looking pictures are often the result, so encourage and reinforce the different looking creations. It is okay if the picture looks completely different from the subject. Discuss the importance of sight. Give time for each participant to reflect and share.

Starry-Night Lights

Materials: Tin cans of any size

Heavy paper

Tape

Old towels or cloths

Hammer and nails

Candles and matches

Prepare the cans by filling them within inch of the top with water and placing them in a freezer until frozen hard (2-3 days). The ice is essential to hold the can firm while the design is being hammered into the metal.

Tape the heavy paper around the frozen cans and draw the desired design unto the paper (each person designs his own). Each participant then will hammer nail holes to make the desired design of holes as traced on the paper. If the ice begins to melt, replace in freezer till hard again. When the design has been completed by hammering holes along the lines, remove the ice, place a candle inside, and enjoy the patterns made by light flickering through the holes. The project is stimulating to visual and kinesthetic sensory perceptions and is also fun. It makes a lovely seasonal project. Turn out lights except for lanterns and share impressions and feelings.

Hillybilly Band

Make rhythm instruments to provide a rare treat for the ears! Some possible instruments are:

Drums—tin cans with plastic lids (bottom cut out), plastic wastebaskets

Shakers—tin cans filled with beans or rice

Thumpers—metal and wood spoons (hit together or on drums)

Bangers—sticks (use on drums)

Cymbals—pot and pan lids

Clappers—wood blocks

Scratchers—sandpaper covered wood blocks

Whoopers—water filled jugs (blow across tops)

Scrapers—thimble and washboard

Gather rhythm instrument materials and make the instruments together. Practice playing with a background tune like "Little Brown Jug". Encourage all efforts.

Tongue Zones

Cut out a picture of a giant tongue from tagboard. On the tongue, identify the parts that receive the following sensations:

    Sweet
    Bitter
    Salty
    Sour

Cut out small pictures of foods and let

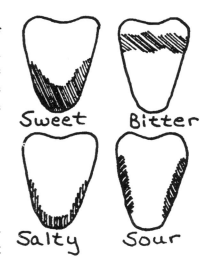

persons take turns drawing food and attaching it to the proper area of the tongue.

Variation: For a more "free wheeling" approach, have them draw pictures of food on the tongue in the correct taste zone, label balloons and attach them to the tongue, or provide samples of each type of food (salty, sweet, bitter and sour) to taste and classify.[8]

Tasty Colors

To explore how color relates to taste, use crayons, pastels, or paint to show primary and secondary colors. Then brainstorm with the group a list of foods related to these colors. Examples might include:

Red:	apple, tomato
Orange:	orange, tangerine, cheese
Yellow:	banana, lemon
Green:	lettuce, cucumber
Blue:	blue cheese
Purple:	plum, eggplant

See how many foods can be associated with each color.[9]

INDIVIDUAL CENTERS

I Hear A Smile

The rhythm of two skipping feet
The lively shout to those I meet

The hands that clap so happily
The whistle of a melody

If I listen for a while
I can really hear a smile[10]

How Does It Feel?

Some things are soft
Like kittens I feel
Some things are hard
Like iron or steel

Some things are hot
Like fire or steam
Some things are cold
Like snow or ice cream[11]

My World Is Real

When I pet a furry cat
soft and purring,
round and fat

When I touch an iron hot
steamy, scary,
full or "not"

When I see a howling wind
blowing, churning
round the bend

When I hear a singing bird
warbling, calling
what I heard

When I feel the snow so cold
icy, crusty
in its hold

When I cuddle in my bed
cozy covers
round my head

Then I know my world is
real
I can tell from all I
feel.

There are also things I
know
I have lived them,
*These are **so**.*

I will live to learn much
more, live to learn
*what life is **for**.*

Face File

Have persons find faces in magazines which show different feelings and mount each face on 8½" x 11" construction paper. Ask them to decide what feeling is described by the face and label the picture. Using heavy dividers, make a file and sort

the faces by feeling categories. Keep the file as a resource for feeling activities such as having persons select a picture from the file to write about or describe on a tape recorder. They can describe the feelings on the face in the picture by answering questions such as: "What part of the face express emotion? Has your face ever looked like this? How do you feel?[12]

This Is Me

Materials: Scissors
Glue
Magazines or
newspapers

Invite each participant to make a collage about himself by gluing special personal items which he likes or which describe him either on the "This Is Me" poster (see end of chapter) or on a plain sheet of paper.

Tasting Centers

1. Provide a shaker of sugar, one of salt, a square of bitter chocolate, and a slice of sour lemon. Let a person taste each, then write or talk about how the tastes are alike and different.

2. Set out bit-size portions of a variety of foods that have different colors and shapes. Let a person match according to shape by grouping together all round, cubical, wedge, cylindrical, or square objects. Now group the objects by color. For example: orange carrots and tangerines, green pickles and celery sticks, yellow cheeses and egg yolks, red radishes and tomatoes, and brown chocolates and coffee. Let him pick one or two and eat.

Smelling Centers

1. Let an individual explore a certain section of a room to discover as many things as possible with different smells. Encourage him to be creative because some things like leather, rubber and wood are apparently odorless, yet do have characteristic smells.

2. Blindfold a person and set out a tray of smelly items. Let him identify them by name after holding and sniffing them.

3. Provide catalogues, magazines or newspapers from which a person can make a collage about things he likes to smell.

4. Provide a spice rack, collection of extracts (such as vanilla, peppermint or spearmint) or a variety of perfumes for an individual to smell. Ask him to sample many of the different smells, and then select his favorite or arrange them in order of preference. He can also write how his nose reacted to so many similar yet different odors.

Seeing Centers

1. Have a discarded or toy camera with which a person can take "pictures". Ask him then to draw pictures of the shots he took with the camera.

2. Provide a shoebox, long strips of paper the width of the box, and two dowels. Let a person draw a story on the paper, and roll it through the shoebox movie screen using the dowels as rolling spindles. Show the homemade movie to the group if desired.

3. Provide an unbreakable hand or wall mirror. Ask the person to write down or tell into a tape recorder everything he sees in the mirror.

4. For visual experiments, combine equal parts of vinegar and baking soda and watch the mixture bubble vigorously. Then dip dirty pennies in a mixture of vinegar and salt, rub them on a cloth, and see the pennies shine like new.

Hearing Centers

1. Let an individual record persons talking or singing on a tape recorder. Have him play back the tape for the group after he has taped a wide selection of sounds.

2. Supply tapes or records with previously recorded sounds such as: sounds around the house (mixer, vacuum cleaner, doorbell, door, toilet, water running, dryer, or washer); sounds of the street (whistle, car, bus, siren, brakes, garbage can clatter, or person shouting). (See "Sound Effects"

Record listed in Appendix). Provide paper and pencil for him to write about each sound.

3. Let a person fill bottles or glasses with various amounts of water. When tapped, these will make different pitches, so he can play tunes or experiment with the different sounds. He may add food coloring.

> Variation: Show a person how to wet his finger and rub it around the rim of the glasses to make another type of tone.

4. Make a double set of sound tubes by filling two tubes with flour, rice, beans, pebbles, salt, a peach-stone, or other noisy ingredients. Let a person shake a container and then find the other container which sounds exactly the same. He may also want to arrange the containers from loudest to softest, or put them in order of which he likes best. Plastic aspirin bottles or metal film cans may be used. Glue all container lids shut when filled.

5. Provide a stethoscope and let a person listen to sounds through it. He may want to find his heartbeat or the heartbeat of another person also.

6. Set out a tray filled with objects that can be used to make such sounds as:

bell	coconut shell	tone block
feather	gong	eggbeater
comb	broom	triangle
tissue	crisp paper	alarm clock
seashell	castanet	tape dispenser

Let a person explore the tray however he desires.

Touching Centers

1. Make or buy a feeling book with the animals or other figures made of various textures such as silk, corduroy, sandpaper, contact paper, cotton, etc. A person can identify the different textures of the materials and describe the different ways they feel to his hand.

2. Let a person explore a variety of items on a touch tray encouraging him to discover how each item feels first with bare hands, and then wearing cotton or rubber gloves. Some possible items are:

   fur (soft, furry)
   pine cone (prickly, rough)

shells (smooth, hard)
plastic (smooth, flexible)
yarn ball (soft, pliable)
rubber foam (spongy, soft)
rope (scratchy, firm)
coil (cold, springy)
bark (rough, bumpy)
wood (smooth, hard)
cactus (prickly, sharp)
sandpaper (scratch, rough)
feather (soft, stiff)
metal (cold, smooth)
brushes (bristly, soft)
fabric (offer variety)
carpet (soft, stiff)
styrofoam (smooth, scratchy)
paper (crisp, smooth)
cellophane (crisp, thin)

3. Make a feel box by preparing a sturdy cardboard box so a person can not see in but can put a hand in through a hole. Put in pairs of matched materials with different textures cut in squares about 4" on a side. Some examples are two pieces of sandpaper, two of velvet, satin, corduroy, plastic, upholstering material, cardboard, carpet squares, formica tiles, cork squares, etc. Persons can reach in and find by feeling the two objects that match.

4. Put one item that can be guessed by touch alone (such as a pencil, crayon, ball, clothespin, string, bottle cap, blunt-nosed scissors, stone, or spoon) into a sack or sock-covered can. Let a person select one of the sacks or cans and see if he can identify the object. Avoid using anything sharp.

5. Group together two alike objects and one different one. Provide several of these collections so a person can pick out the different one in each set. The objects can be alike in color and shape, but one will be different in texture.

BOOKS

Picture Books

Alike, Diogenes (Brandenberg, Aliki), **My Five Senses.**
Allington, Richard and Kathleen Cowles
    Feelings.
    Hearing.
    Looking.
    Smelling.
    Tasting.
    Touching.
Andersen, Hans Christian, **The Ugly Duckling.**
Bishop, Claire and Kurt Weise, **The Five Chinese Brothers.**
Brenner, Barbara, **Faces.**
Brown, Marc Tolan, **Arthur's Eyes.**
Brown, Margaret Wise, **The Important Book.**
Elkin, Benjamin, **The Loudest Mouse In The World.**
Ets, Marie H., **Gilberto And The Wind.**
Gay, Zhenya, **Look.**
Geisel, Theodore Seuss, **The Foot Book.**
Hoban, Tana, (Wordless), **Look Again.**
Holzenthaler, Jean, **My Feet Do.**
Holzenthaler, Jean, **My Hands Can.**
Kauffman, Lois, **What's The Noise?**
Krauss, Ruth, **The Growing Story.**
Kuskin, Karla, **Roar And More.**
Kuskin, Karla, **Square As A House.**
Kionni, Leo, **Fish Is Fish.**
Kionni, Leo, **Tico And The Golden Wings.**
Panek, Dennis, **Matilda Hippo Has A Big Mouth.**
Schlein, Miriam, **Shapes.**
Showers, Paul, **Find Out By Touching.**
Showers, Paul, **Follow Your Nose.**
Showers, Paul, **How Many Teeth.**
Showers, Paul, **The Listening Walk.**
Showers, Paul, **Look At Your Eyes.**
Tudor, Tasha, **First Delights: A Book About The Five Senses.**
Waber, Bernard, **You Look Ridiculous.**

Fiction Books

Feist, Julia, **Look Who's Beautiful.**
Perl, Lila, **Hey, Remember Fat Glenda?**
Philips, Barbara, **Don't Call Me Fatso.**
Robison, Nancy Louise, **Ballet Magic.**

Footnotes

[1] Joyce King and Carol Katzman, Imagine That (Santa Monica, California: Goodyear Publishing Co., 1976), p. 125.

[2] John O. Stevens, Awareness (Lafayette, California: Real People Press, 1971), p. 243.

[3] *Ibid.*, p. 14.

[4] King, p. 55.

[5] Valerie Sloane, Creative Family Activities (Nashville, Tennessee: Parthenon Press, 1976), p. 30.

[6] King, p. 52.

[7] *Ibid.*, p. 51.

[8] *Ibid.*, p. 63.

[9] *Ibid.*

[10] *Ibid.*, p. 82

[11] *Ibid.*, p. 50

[12] *Ibid.*, p. 92.

This is Me!

Cut out words and pictures from magazines and newspapers that describe yourself.

Arrange and paste them on this page.

CHAPTER 2

Awareness Of Feelings

INTRODUCTION OF CONCEPT

All humans experience feelings and emotions. Most of us make value judgments about feelings, categorizing them as "bad" or "good". Feelings and emotions are facts of life. It is the way we deal with and cope with the feelings that hinders or helps us, keeps us moral and ethical or not, and enhances or destroys our sensitivities to others.

The feelings we have which are not recognized or identified remain unacknowledged, unaccepted, and unprocessed. These are powerful and potentially dangerous to the person who bottles them up and holds them inside (does not express the feelings). Ignored emotions do not resolve themselves. Emotions lacking appropriate channels and expressions may be expressed in painful actions or be exposed unconsciously through physical symptoms of illness. Whether an individual's coping pattern is to fight, to run, or to submit, unnamed feelings are often a powerful influence over our behaviors and beliefs. Recognized emotions are more manageable and are readily accessible for conscious monitoring. What we can name, we begin to acknowledge, accept, and process. We can name, work on, and take responsibility for feelings that we have access to and thus disarm potentially damaging feelings.

Children are not often encouraged to recognize their own feelings. They are often discounted or punished when they express unpleasant or embarrassing emotions. We can help them accept themselves and their emotions by our own modeling of *unconditional acceptance, mutual respect,* and *taking the child seriously.* If a child indicates fear, believe that emotion because the child is the only one who really knows.

Children do, in fact, have the capacity for the entire range of emotions that adults experience and feel. Children often do not have the language of emotions that some adults have. If a child feels ugly and says so, *listen* (see Chapter 7) and respect those feelings rather than insisting that the child's judgment is wrong. As children gain experience in naming and accepting their emotions, they will become better equipped to express their feelings appropriately and to recognize and respect the feelings of others.

As children find names for their emotions, they will also gain control and understanding over the emotions that most often precede anger. This one self-understanding tool enables self-control much beyond most peoples' expectations of themselves and others.

INTRODUCTION TO PARTICIPANTS

As we have been living inside our body houses today, we have probably felt many things through our sense of touch: the blankets when we slid out of bed this morning, the wetness of water when we washed, and the surfaces on which we are sitting now. (ASK FOR OTHER FEELINGS.) A special different kind of feeling is called an "emotion". Every day we feel the emotions which come and go through our bodies. Let us take time to name as many "feeling emotions" as we can remember.

(SEE LISTING OF FEELINGS IN THE APPENDIX AND REVIEW THEM WITH THE YOUTH.)

When we feel these emotions, it is as if someone turned our inside temperature up or down a lot more than usual. Sometimes we feel like an emotion fills our body houses with smoke and turns up the temperature very high. We may call this "losing my temper" or "getting mad". When this happens, we may do things we would not otherwise do. Which emotions feel "hot" to you? What kinds of things have you seen people do when they are angry? Which are nice and warm or pleasantly cool feelings?

(ALLOW TIME FOR DISCUSSION.)

If we look to see what it is that turns up the heat or makes the smoke just before we get angry, we discover something. We do not just "get" mad. Something happens earlier which hurts, frightens, or embarrasses us, and THEN we feel the heat of anger or being mad. Notice that anger is always the second emotion, not the first step in what happens. Think about the last time you were really angry! What was the very first thing which happened that turned up your heat? Did you get worried, hurt, scared, or embarrassed? That was your first emotion. Being angry or mad was the second emotion. We will try to spot these first emotions before they get to our thermostat and we feel hot or angry.

Emotions are not bad or good by themselves. Sometimes the things we do to clear out the heat and smoke can be very good or bad. We will learn the names of our many emotions so we can take care of them before they can take control of us. We may learn the names and get in touch with some emotions which are new to us. If so, we will know ourselves better and be more able to live peaceably with ourselves, our families, and our neighbors.

INTERACTION ACTIVITIES

What Are They Feeling?

Purpose; to show that everyone has feelings and that this is normal and okay. To encourage participants to identify their own feelings.

Select pictures from magazines or posters (or have participants do so) which portray strong feelings through facial expressions, body language, or situational scenes. Cut out and mount if desired, or ask participants to do so. Try to find many age levels in the pictures to demonstrate that people of all ages experience all kinds of feelings. Select negative as well as positive feelings.

Post, hold up, or otherwise display one picture at a time or pass them around if the group is too large. Invite participants to give their opinions as to what feelings or emotion is being pictured. Ask questions as:

1. What kinds of feelings might this person be experiencing?

2. How do you think you might feel in this situation?

3. What might have happened just before this picture was taken of drawn?

4. What might have happened just after?

5. Have you ever felt like that? Would you like to tell

us about it?

6. What happened before you felt that way?

When I See That Picture I Feel...

Materials: Color pictures and photographs showing scenes such as:

> a colorful day
> a wintry day
> a dismal, dreary landscape
> a bright and cheerful scene
> a cheery, indoor setting

(Try to secure scenes without people)

Hold pictures up one at a time for the persons to see. Invite them to comment. Encourage them to look at the colors and ask what feelings they associate with them.

Now have them observe how the artist used her brush strokes. Do they go up or down? Are the lines straight or crooked? Notice the thick or thin paint and the gentle or hard lines.

Do you respond differently to differing techniques? Comment on the movement in the pictures. Ask questions such as:

> "What do you think is happening to the leaves in this picture?"

> "What is moving?"

> "Why is the girl's hair back like that? What makes your hair do that?"

Note other shapes in the pictures. Ask:

> "How do you think this would feel—round or flat?"

> "How did the artist make this look round instead of flat?"

Note the texture within the pictures. Ask:

> "Do you think this is rough or smooth?"

> "Why does it look rough or smooth?"

Variation: Try showing works by famous artists who used distinctive styles to achieve specific results, such as Vincent Van Gogh, Andrew Wyeth or Claude Monet.

Trust Walk

Have the group pair off and blindfold one person in each team. Instruct the sighted person to take the blindfold one on a walk. Remind her to watch for steps, obstacles, and dangers for the "blind" person. Have them switch roles half way through the walk. When they return, discuss feelings involved in being responsible for one another, and learning to trust a partner.

Make Up A Story

Invite participants to sit in a circle and take turns throwing a single die. Post a "Make Up a Story" list with six different instructions, one for each number on the die,

"Make Up a Story" in which you...

1. are the star and everything you do is super.
2. escape from a dangerous situation.
3, are very afraid of something.
4. experience something very beautiful.
5. something exciting and wonderful happens.
6. hear, see or touch something important.

Invite participants to throw the die and follow the instructions corresponding to the number rolled. Encourage persons to be creative, exaggerate, and surprise the listeners. Create an atmosphere of acceptance in which all efforts are rewarded with positive feedback.

Stepping Stones

Ask each person to write down the five most important events (stepping stones) in her life so far. These can be events which have changed her the most, or through which she has grown. Allow some time to think and write. Then ask her to share either with a partner or with the group.

Variations:

1. Ask a person to share about one stepping stone of her choice.

2. Ask individuals to chart the events high or low depending on how the experience felt at the time, and then chart them again high or low depending on how she sees them now and what effects these events have had on her life.

3. Ask individuals to do stepping stones at home and bring them to the group to share.

Personal Journals

Supply each person with a notebook and pencil. Allow time for each to write down personal reactions either to a previous discussion or to questions you ask them. Encourage persons to take these notebooks home and use them as personal journals, or keep them in the room for use as a part of the group experience.

Reflections Calendar

My Reflections for the Month of _____ , _____

Sunday	Monday	Tuesday	Wednesday	Thursday	Friday	Saturday
			If only . . .		When I . . . I feel good	
	I want to remember . . .				Today I feel . . .	
		Today is important because . . .		I want to be . . .		
	I like it when . . .		A nice thing happened today . . .		I'm happy that . . .	
		I want to remember . . .			Sometimes I feel . . .	

Look at the reflections calendar poster (see posters at the end of chapter). Provide each person with her own poster and with a regular calendar which shows the dates. Have her fill in the correct numbers on the reflections calendar so it will correspond to the current month. Invite her to decorate the calendar, take it home, and answer the questions on the days indicated. She may write her answers in a journal or bring them to the group to discuss.

Things I Do Well

Have each person make a list entitled "Five things I can do well". Let all who are willing share from their lists and encourage the group to add comments about what their friends do well. Now make a second list entitled "Five things I wish I could do better". Discuss with the group the balance between their present abilities and their future goals. Reinforce self- encouragements and positive strokes by others.

✝ ✝ ✝ ✝

I Am Like...

Let each person answer the question "I am like what animal?", and explain her reasons for the choice. This helps persons identify and share interesting characteristics about themselves. Other categories besides animals can be used for variety such as plants, cars, foods, etc. Invite participants to express feelings about their animals.

✝ ✝ ✝ ✝

Who Am I?

Materials: One sheet of paper for each
                    person
                    Pencils
                    Straight pins

Pass out paper and pencils, and instruct each participant to write five to ten different answers to the question "Who Am I?" When everyone is done, ask them to pin their answers to the front of their clothes, and to circulate in the group *without speaking*. They are to make eye contact with each person they encounter, and then to read each other's answers to the question. After a few minutes, explain that they may now return to anyone they though would be interesting

to talk to, and ask questions of each other.

Variations: Persons may draw pictures of themselves instead of answering the questions, or they may draw pictures of some animal or object with which to identify.

✝ ✝ ✝ ✝

Similarities And Differences

To explore the ways in which people are alike, ask the group to brainstorm on the question "In what ways am I like someone else?" Write down all ideas, and give suggestions such as we all have ears, thoughts, dreams, etc.

Now list ways in which people differ from each other. Suggest differences such as foot sizes, favorite sports, interests, etc. Allow time for all to contribute. Display the two lists and ask questions of the group such as:

1. When do you try to be like someone else?

2. When do you really want to be different from everybody else?

3. What are some of your reasons for wanting to be like someone else?

4. What are some of your reasons for wanting to be different?

5. What are some ways you are similar to others in this group?

6. What are some ways you are different from others in this group?

7. What would our group be like if everyone in it were exactly alike?

8. What would our group be like if everyone were completely different?

The purpose of this activity is to help persons appreciate individual differences and become aware of similarities within their group.

✝ ✝ ✝ ✝

"Ten Activities I Enjoy Doing"

Materials: paper and pencil

Instruct each participant to make a list of ten activities she enjoys doing.

When the lists are completed, instruct the participants to:

1. Number activities in the order of their priority to the participant (e.g. #1 most important, #2 etc.)

2. Code each activity with:

"S" if it costs more than $5.00

"P" if other people are needed to participate

"A" if activity can be done alone; and write the date of the most recent time the activity has been engaged in by the participant.

When writing is completed, discuss hows and whys of the choices.

Variation: pin or tape the sheet as "name tag"; walk around sharing and noting similarities and differences. Use "get-acquainted" triads or larger groups. Talk about the experience in the group.

✛ ✛ ✛ ✛

Describe Your Values

Invite participants to think about one person (other than themselves) with whom they are comfortable and with whom they like to spend time. Ask them to write or tell three words to describe the person. Ask them to think of someone with whom they are uncomfortable and with whom they do not like to spend time. Ask them to write or tell three words to describe that person.

List all the "uncomfortable" words in one column; the "comfortable" words in another. Post these lists and discuss for insight and understanding.

✛ ✛ ✛ ✛

Choice Changes

Select questions which suit the age of the participants and read them one by one. Instruct participants to raise one hand if their vote is "yes", to turn thumbs down if "no", and to cross their arms if they cannot decide. Each participant makes decisions during the activity and sees others also making value choices. After enough statements have been read to show differ-

ences, divide into groups and invite each person to explain why she believes and feels as she does about the statements. Participants may question each other or try to influence, but are to avoid "put-downs" or name calling. Help them learn to accept differences of opinion.

How many of you:

1. _____ have one or more pets at home?

2. _____ wish you were the only child in your family?

3. _____ sometimes feel afraid in the dark?

4. _____ like to take trips in the car?

5. _____ would like to go to bed later at night than you now do?

6. _____ like one TV show better than any other?

7. _____ would change your name if you could?

8. _____ like to swim?

9. _____ would live in a different city if you had a chance?

10. _____ would live on a farm if you had the opportunity?

11. _____ would live in another country if you had a chance?

12. _____ would like to stay by yourself on a deserted island for three days or more?

13. _____ buy or select your own clothes? decide what you will wear each day?

14. _____ have an older brother or sister?

15. _____ wake yourself up in the morning?

16. _____ have visited the place where your mother or father works?

17. _____ know someone of the opposite sex with whom you like to spend time?

18. _____ would like to be on a "first name" basis with your teacher?

19. _____ feel uncomfortable when your friends and your parents meet?

20. _____ feel comfortable in telling your parents about your personal problems?

21. _____ would keep on going to school if it weren't required?

22. _____ have a fantasy sometimes about being famous or very rich?

23. _____ feel hurt when someone gives you criticism?

24. _____ try to hide your feelings if you are angry?

25. _____ have had a broken bone?

26. _____ made Christmas gifts yourself for family or friends?

27. _____ have felt "left out" at some time?

28. _____ think that you are fairly organized as a person?

29. _____ know what is in the top drawer of your dresser?

30. _____ have been angry enough to wish you could hurt someone for something they have done?

31. _____ would like to belong to a different family?

32. _____ have ever been in the room when someone died?

33. _____ have ever seen a dead person?

34. _____ have religion as an important value to you?

35. _____ would like to change yourself in some way?

36. _____ have a special hobby or something you like to do whenever you can?

37. _____ think that cheating is sometimes okay?

38. _____ have some secrets you wouldn't tell anyone?

39. _____ have fun with your family?

40. _____ are wearing socks?

41. _____ have a hole in a sock today?

42. _____ have awakened from a dream feeling afraid?

43. _____ have felt hurt by something a friend did?

44. _____ would you vote for a law which said families could have no more than two children?

45. _____ think that women should not work outside the home?

46. _____ have ever seen persons of different races fighting one another?

47. _____ have ever eaten yogurt?

48. _____ would like to try sky-diving?

49. _____ like to go on walks?

50. _____ think you may have been in love?

51. _____ have felt alone, even though a lot of people were around?

52. _____ play some musical instrument?

53. _____ read the newspaper other than the funnies?

54. _____ have finished a book in the last month?

55. _____ find it hard to concentrate on what another person is saying at times?

Variation: Construct a "choice continuum" or "barometer" line from 0-100 or 1-10 which extends across the room (10 area is highly agree: 1 area is strongly disagree). Ask participants to place themselves on the line according to their beliefs and feelings in reaction to the questions which ask for opinions. Pause between the reading of the statements long enough for each participant to place herself and to note where others in the group place themselves. No one is to try to influence where another places herself. Discuss in small groups.

"Act It Out"

Invite participants to select everyday experiences and act them out in pantomime, emphasizing the feelings that go with experiences. Demonstrate with a starter such as "Think of an array of your favorite fruits set out for you to select and buy. There are bananas, grapes, apples, peaches, nectarines, anything you like. Now, let's act out the selection of just exactly the right piece of fruit—but only act it—no words. Check it all out when you have found just what you want, pantomime the process of getting it ready to eat. Peel it, wash it, or whatever you need to do. Show your feelings still more as you pantomime eating it—or perhaps it did not taste as you expected—or you dropped it. Negative feelings are okay too.

Brainstorm together and let participants act out other experiences which bring out feelings (e.g. spilling a glass of milk and cleaning it up; selecting flowers for a bouquet; scrubbing down bathroom fixtures).

Act Out Feelings

Divide into small groups. Set a scene for each group, ask them to decide who will act out each part, and how the scene will end. Give them time to practice and then ask each group to act out their scene for the big group. Discuss how each character in the skit was feeling, and how the actors felt in their roles.

Possible scenes:

1. You have just arrived on the school ground, and it is the first day of school. There is no one in sight whom you know. You are alone.

2. You are on a field trip with your group to a big factory. Your shoe comes untied, you reach down to tie it and it won't tie. When you finally get it fixed, your group is nowhere in sight.

3. You just received a big test back from the teacher. You received a low grade and you had studied hard. The teacher is walking toward you.

Frustration Fantasies

Ask each person to think of a situation which is frustrating to her. Tell your own personal frustration to encourage participation and to give them ideas. Let it be something which happens enough to be regularly bothersome. It may be big, perfumey aunts who always want to hug and kiss you, or perhaps someone who tells you that she will do something, and doesn't follow through. Whatever is a frustration for you is appropriate.

Divide into groups of not more than four persons. Give each group a fairly private space and explain to them that each person in the group is to have a turn to act out her frustration with everyone else helping. But in the end, it can turn out the way the person with the frustration desires rather than the way it usually does. For instance, in the case of the perfumey aunt, the person can have one of her group members be the aunt who does the gushy thing and she can say what she has always wanted to say to the aunt. Each person gets her turn. The rest of the group helps her make it happen. Stress confidentiality. Persons may share their frustration fantasies, but not another person's with the whole group.

Charades—A Feeling Message

Prepare and place in a container a list of feeling charade topics (engage the participants in writing a charade which would be useful to act out after they have seen the idea demonstrated and played for a short time). Each topic is to be on a separate, small sheet of paper. Some possible feeling charade topics would be:

I am happy	I am proud	I am pleased
I am sad	I am ashamed	I am upset
I am furious	I am discouraged	I am
I am embarrassed	I am angry	determined
I am scared	I am hurt	I am concerned
		I am bored

Invite participants to divide themselves into two teams and count off. Player #1 on the first team takes a message out of the box, then acts out the message in pantomime or "charade talk" to her team. Members of the other team do not speak. Each player is allowed one minute to act out her message so that team members get the idea and say it. If they do not succeed, the other team is to try. Score one point for the team which states the message within the time limit. Extend the limit if one minute does not seem long enough for the group, but keep it the same for both groups. Encourage lots of body language, enthusiasm, and spontaneous guessing from the teams.

Repeat the process with team #2, first player, drawing and acting out for her team. If scoring and timing seem to inhibit, just play the game for pure fun and encourage participants to posture, gesture, and use all kinds of facial expressions. This gives experience in trying new role models and allowing spontaneity about feelings expressed.

For younger children simplify the messages and give hints to the actors as to how they can better express the feelings.

Interpret Feelings

Brainstorm or use the feeling list (see Appendix) to generate a full list of feelings. Write them one at a time where everyone can see, call out the specific feeling as you write it, and invite persons to interpret that feeling through dance, body posture, expression, or other media of your choice.

Variation: Ask persons to dance, draw, or act out the feeling they feel at the particular moment.

ARTS AND CRAFTS

Feeling Collage

Provide magazines or catalogues, and ask each person to find one picture to contribute to the group's collage. These pictures can depict persons showing emotions such as anger, fear, shame, joy or sorrow. Overlap and glue the pictures to one large sheet of paper. Use black markers to outline and give puzzle effect to the divided edges, or tear the pictures out and leave the edges rough for a blended look. Label the emotions shown in the pictures, and discuss feelings with the group.

My Collection Of Feeling Words

Invite each participant to think of many words which describe feelings and emotions and to write them down with simple drawings or cut-out pictures to illustrate. Supply materials to make a simple book which can be added to as the individual becomes aware of new feelings and emotions.

Patchwork Quilt Of Faces

Provide pieces of colored construction paper about 6" square and ask persons to use markers to draw a face representing a feeling they have had: Happiness, Sadness, Frustration, Pain, Love, or others. Tape or glue the squares together to make a feeling quilt.[1]

Feelings Mobile

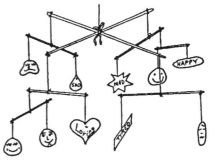

Give persons wire coat hangers or wooden dowels, and ask them to tie string to parts of the hanger and attach cards with their feelings written on them. Pictures may be drawn on the back of cards to illustrate the feelings. A paper circle with a face drawn on it can be mounted on top of the hanger or in the center of the dowel to show one of the person's expressions.[2]

My Group And Me

After the first meeting of a group, before dismissal, provide newsprint and magic markers. Invite participants to mark off the newsprint into blocks, one for each session. Post all the sheets and encourage each participant to picture or use words to portray her relationship to the group at the end of each session. Discuss and accept all responses.

"Pictures Of My Life"

Provide participants with paper and pencil. Invite them to draw lines to divide the paper into twelve or less equal-sized section. Instruct participants to use simple pictures, symbols, and/or words to portray an important event in their lives (or in the life of the group) within each section. Encourage them with starters such as "This is a picture of the time when…" or "I'll always remember when…"

✛ ✛ ✛ ✛

Warm/Cold: Positive/Negative

Invite the participants to select two sheets of colored paper; one full size (8½ x 11) a light color they see as warm and friendly, the other a dark color they see as cold and distant (half sheet).

Ask them to fold the smaller (dark) sheet in half, pencil a design on the folded side, and cut it out (the design section which has been cut out represents warm, positive feelings).

Demonstrate how to unfold both parts and past the section which has been cut out onto one half of the full sheet of warm bright colored paper. The section con-

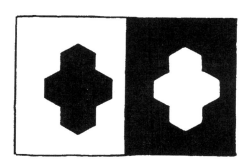

taining the cut-out design (hole) is to be pasted on the other half of the bright colored sheet.

"Positive" and "negatives" of the same image are thus created. Discuss positive/negative and warm/cold feelings with the participants. Involve the colors used and what feelings they represent to the participant.

Ask which feelings they think are positive and which negative. Ask how they deal with both kinds of feelings. What happens? Encourage open discussion.

✛ ✛ ✛ ✛

All About Me (A Pictorial Autobiography)

Materials: Plain paper
Crayons, colored pencils
   or markers
String
Hole punch
Magazines, newspapers,
   catalogues
Glue or tape

Help each person begin her "All About Me" book by having her draw or cut out pictures which illustrate such things as her ideal home, a friend, favorite foods, favorite stories, what she likes to do best, or pictures which remind her of herself. Attach each picture or group of pictures to a plain sheet with glue or tape, label, punch holes for attaching and tie together with yarn, string, or other fasteners. This will create an "All About Me" book.

✛ ✛ ✛ ✛

A Reflection Of Me

Show persons how to attach a small pocket mirror with glue to the inside of the lid of a shoe box. Suggest that they decorate the inside of the lid with symbols that reflect their interests and personalities. Encourage individual expression such as: a thumb print (each person's is different); pictures brought from home; cut out magazine pictures of foods, sports, and hobbies of interest to the person, etc.

When the inside of the lid is decorated they may wrap the outside edges with heavy yarn and use glue to hold the yard in place if they desire. A large loop of yarn can be attached at one end to hang the lid. Each person now has a picture to hang which reflects herself.[3]

✛ ✛ ✛ ✛

Birthday Graph

On a large sheet of poster board, write the names of the months in a column on the left side. Use an appropriate color and symbol for each month. Give each person in the group her own "cut-out cake" on which to record her name and date of birth. Place the "birthday cakes" next to the appropriate months. Discuss how each person has a special day to celebrate because each person is important and special.[4]

✛ ✛ ✛ ✛

Group Photo Album

Materials: photograph of each person
colored construction paper
paper punch
yarn or string

Have each person bring a photograph of herself to the group meeting or use a Polaroid camera and take pictures of each person. Make an album out of construction paper by punching holes in the pages and tying them together with yarn or string. The group can decorate the cover of the album. Glue each person's picture on a page and let them print or write their names under it. Other themes can be added to the book such as group accomplishments or discussion topics if desired.

My Own Bulletin Board

Give each participant an opportunity to create a bulletin board about herself. Ask her to find pictures which show her interests, likes, family information, or any other material that will help others understand her as a unique individual. Assist her in arranging and attaching her materials onto the bulletin board. Provide markers, magazines, pictures, paper, letter forms, and other supplies as desired.

Compare Pictures

Have each person draw a picture of the most beautiful, or funniest, or most frightening thing she has ever seen. Have all persons draw on the same topic, and then let each tell about her picture. Each picture will be different, though all started from the same idea. Discuss how each person's ideas and values can differ and still be acceptable.

Suggestion Pictures

Provide a sheet of paper for each participant which has a figure or "picture suggestion" on it. Invite participants to complete a picture allowing the figures to  suggest a subject, and be utilized as a part of the picture. Compare the final pictures and discuss each person's unique way of developing her picture. Guide the discussion toward valuing each individual's creation for its own special ideas. Invite each participant to interpret her picture.

 (center divider)

I-Land Visit

Give each person in the group a piece of newsprint or butcher paper about 3 feet square. On this, ask them to draw their own island and put on the island anything they desire. Encourage them to think what kind of fruit they might grow on their islands, what kind of terrain is there, what the products of their islands are, what kind of weather they have, etc. Suit the activity to your age level.

Variation: Set aside a time each week for visits to the islands, and suggest additions to be made each time. Work toward "I" message lesson.

Make A Puzzle

Invite each participant to choose a favorite picture from a magazine, poster, calendar, etc. to make into a puzzle. Demonstrate how to glue the pictures onto cardboard (cereal boxes are a good source of the right weight of cardboard) and trim the edges. Cut the puzzle into as many pieces as desired. Place each set of  puzzle pieces into a separate envelope or box to take home. Listen and reflect individual's feelings about their project.

Variation: Invite participants to choose only pictures showing emotion. Discuss with starters such as: "When I look at my picture I feel…", or "This picture reminds me of…"

Name Design

Invite participants to take a sheet of paper, fold it down the center, and then use crayons to inscribe their 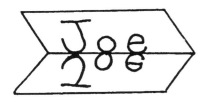 names along the fold line, pressing hard on the crayon. Refold the paper, rub and open. A "reverse" design appears. Encourage creative use of color combinations. Discuss the beauty and uniqueness of each person as represented in this activity.

INDIVIDUAL CENTERS

I Feel...

Provide magazines or catalogs from which a person may cut pictures to show how she feels at the moment. She may then glue them onto a large sheet of paper and hang them as desired. This activity can give the person a chance to ventilate her feelings. If someone is expressing strong emotions, give her an active situation in which to ventilate her feelings such as talking to an active listener.

✛ ✛ ✛ ✛

Personal Weather Reports

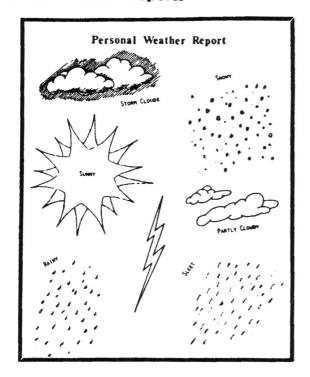
Personal Weather Report

Post a large sheet of newsprint or butcher paper on the wall with each group member's name written on it. Encourage individuals to go to the weather station as they choose and to post their own weather reports. They may either write words to describe how they are feeling that day, or tape weather symbols beside their name (see poster at end of chapter). Through the day, let persons change their weather reports as their feelings change. Allow persons to explain their weather if they desire.

Variation: Reproduce the poster and invite each person to chart her own weather report over a given period of time. Discuss with acceptance!

✛ ✛ ✛ ✛

Feelings Clock

Instruct an individual to think back over the past few hours and remember how she felt each hour. She can label the hours on the Feeling Clock (see poster at end of chapter) and draw scenes portraying situations in which she had strong feelings, or use symbols representing the feelings. If her feelings fluctuated within

Feelings Clock

the hour, she may show that in her picture also. Be sure to let the person create her own method for showing the feelings that day. Discuss how feelings fluctuate and how persons can learn to better control their change through naming, owning and expressing them.

✛ ✛ ✛ ✛

Feelings Centers

Provide individual centers in semi-private places which are each oriented around one specific feeling such as a happy center, an angry center, an embarrassed center, or a lonely center. Decorate the center with pictures showing that emotion.

Encourage persons to leave group activities to spend time in a feeling center when they are currently experiencing that specific emotion. In the center they can write about their emotions (provide paper and pencils), tape them on a tape recorder (supply the tape recorder, blank tape and instructions for taping and erasing), form them in clay (have an open surface, container for water, and some clay), or paint them on paper (supply paper, paints and an old shirt).

Try various kinds of centers to find what works best. Use other media if desired.

✝ ✝ ✝ ✝

Personal Information Posters

These thirteen posters (see posters at end of chapter) can be completed and decorated by an individual. They are designed to affirm that the individual is unique and important by asking for her personal information and ideas. The topics are:

1. Who Am I?—information about age, height, birth date, shoe size, etc.

2. This Is Me—characteristics of my face

3. My Name Is—personal data about my name, address, birthday, etc.

4. My Hands and Feet—questions about my hands and feet

5. My Feelings—questions about what feelings I have and when I have them

6. More Me—things I like, my animals, and my eating habits

7. My Family—draw a portrait of my family

8. My Family Autographs—family signatures and pet's paw print

9. My Room, My House—questions about where I live

10. My Neighborhood Map—questions about the area around my house

11. My Town Autographs—signatures of people in my town

12. Friends, Sports—questions about my best friend, favorite teacher, favorite sports, etc.

13. Working—Survey of those working at my house, and of what their jobs require

As a person completes several of these posters, they can be bound together into a personal information book.[5]

BOOKS

Picture Books

Ancona, George, **I Feel.**
Anglund, Joan, **Do You Love Someone?**
Anglund, Joan, **Love Is A Special Way Of Feeling.**
Anglund, Joan, **What Color Is Love?**
Blume, Judy, **Otherwise Known As Sheila The Great.**
Blume, Judy, **The Pain And The Great One.**
Dana, Barbara, **Zucchini.**
De Paola, Thomas Anthony, **Andy (That's My Name).**
Duvoisin, Roger A., **Veronica.**
Flack, Marjorie, **Ask Mister Bear.**
Freeman, Don, **Dandelion.**
Gay, Zhenya, **What's Your Name?**
Hughes, Shirley, **Moving Molly.**
Jenkins, Jordan, **Learning About Love.**
Keats, Ezra J., **Whistle For Willie.**
Kent, Jack, **The Wizard Of Wallaby Wallow.**
Klagsbrun, Francine, Ed., **Free To Be… You And Me.**
Leaf, Munro, **The Story Of Ferdinand.**
Leaf, Munro, **Who Cares? I Do.**
Martin, Bill Jr., **Brown Bear, Brown Bear, What Do You See?**
Martin, Bill Jr., **David Was Mad.**
Moncure, Jane Belk, **Love.**
Mosel, Arlene, **Tikki Tikki Tembo.**
Sharmar, Marjorie Weinman, **Rollo And Juliet, Forever.**
Simon, Norma, **How Do I Feel?**
Simon, Norma, **I Was So Mad?**
Stone, Elberta, **I'm Glad I'm Me.**

Fiction Books

De Angeli, Marguerite, L., **Bright April.**
Desbarats, Peter, **Gabrielle & Selena.**
Flory, Jane, **One Hundred And Eight Bells.**
Greene, Constance C., **The Unmaking Of Rabbit.**
Hamilton, Virginia, **Zeely.**
Hogan, Paula, **Sometimes I Get So Mad.**
Hunter, Edith Fisher, **Sue Ellen.**
Park, Barbara, **Don't Make Me Smile.**
Sachs, Marilyn, **Mary.**
Skolsky, Mindy Warshaw, **Carnival And Kopeck And More About Hannah.**
Stanek, Muriel Novella, **Who's Afraid Of The Dark?**
Teible, Margaret, **Davey Comes Home.**

Footnotes

[1]Joyce King and Carol Katzman, Imagine That (Santa Monica, California: Goodyear Publishing Co., 1976), p. 92.

[2]*Ibid.*, p. 107

[3]*Ibid.*, p. 94.

[4]*Ibid.*, p. 146.

[5]Clover Club Wichita (Wichita, Kansas: Sedgwick County Extension Service), p. 2-13.

My Reflections for the Month of _____

Sunday	Monday	Tuesday	Wednesday	Thursday	Friday	Saturday
			If only...		When I... I feel good	
	I want to remember...				Today I feel....	
		Today is important because...		I want to be ...		
	I like it when....		A nice thing happened today....		I'm happy that....	
		I want to remember ...			Sometimes I feel....	

Personal Weather Report

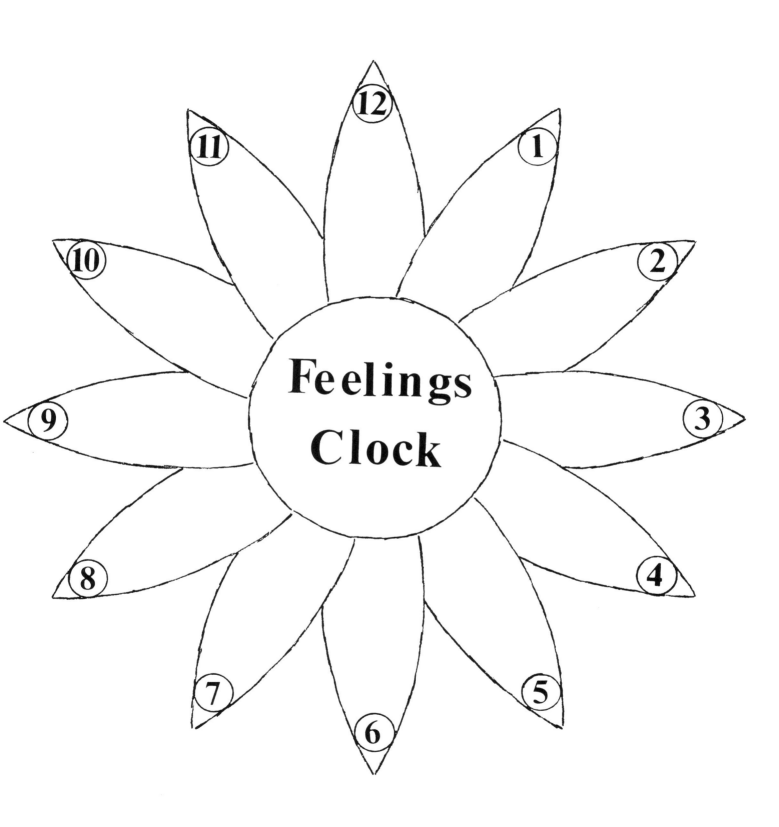

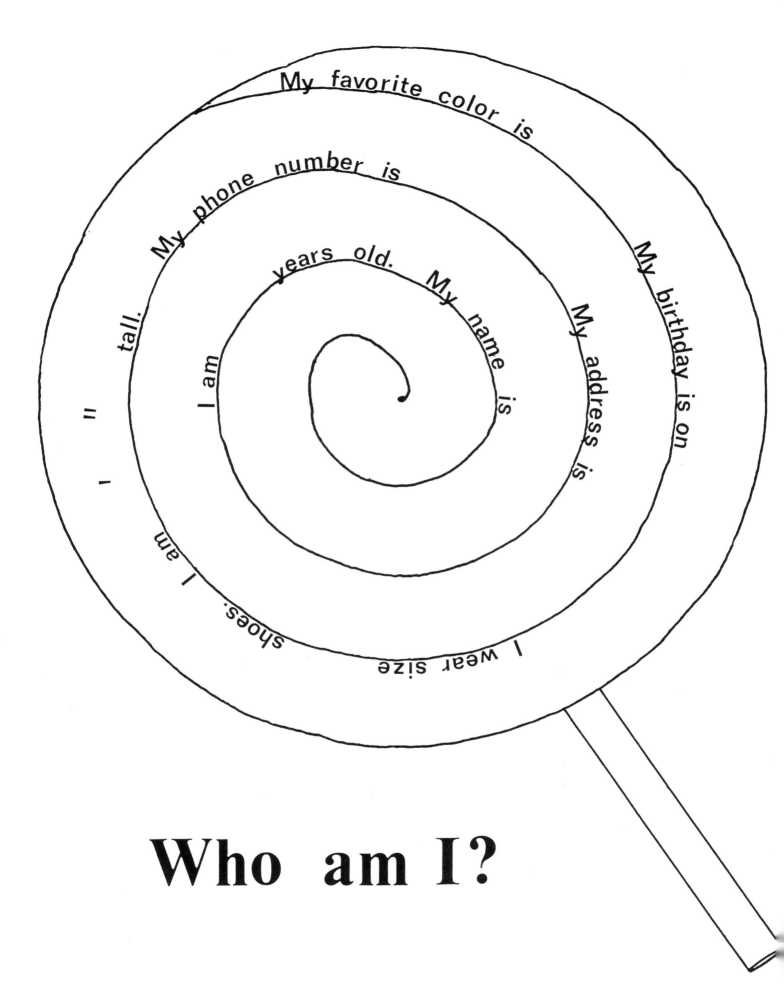

My favorite color is

My phone number is

My birthday is on

tall.

years old. My name is

I am

My address is

I

I wear size

shoes, I am

Who am I?

THIS IS ME

MY HAIR
(I DREW IT)

MY EYES ARE
_____
(COLOR)

I WEAR FRECKLES

☐ YES   ☐ NO

I HAVE ____ TEETH
(NUMBER)

CLOVER CLUB WICHITA

Sedg. Co. Extension Service
9000 W. Central
722-7721

MY NAME IS _____

I AM A ☐ BOY ☐ GIRL

MY ADDRESS IS:

POSTCARD

_____

_____

_____

_____ ZIP _____

MY BIRTHDAY IS:

MONTH _____

DAY _____

YEAR _____

I AM ____ YEARS OLD

CLOVER CLUB
WICHITA

Sedg. Co. Extension Service
9000 W. Central
722-7721

MY HANDS AND FEET

THIS IS MY HAND ⬆
(I TRACED IT)

I AM LEFTHANDED ☐
RIGHTHANDED ☐

MY FEET ARE TICKLISH
☐ YES   ☐ NO

MY FEELINGS

SOMETIMES I
FEEL SCARED
☐ YES ☐ NO
WHEN I'M
SCARED I
_____
_____

SOMETIMES I CRY
☐ YES ☐ NO

I FEEL THE
SADDEST WHEN
_____
_____

I'M HAPPY
☐ ALL THE TIME
☐ MOST THE TIME
☐ NEVER

WHAT MAKES
ME HAPPIEST IS
_____
_____

SOMETIMES I GET
MAD AT PEOPLE.
☐ YES ☐ NO
I GET THE
MADDEST WHEN
_____
_____

THINGS I LIKE

MY FAVORITE ANIMAL IS _____

MY SECOND FAVORITE IS _____

I OWN ONE ☐

I OWN BOTH ☐

I DON'T OWN EITHER ☐   I WISH I DID ☐

IF I COULD BE AN ANIMAL I'D BE A

_____   _____

ANIMALS

EATING

I EAT LIKE A   ☐ HOG   ☐ BIRD   ☐ _____

MY FAVORITE FOOD IS _____

BUT I CAN'T STAND _____

MY MOTHER THINKS I SHOULD LIKE _____

(BUT I DON'T.)

MY FAMILY

(I DREW THIS PICTURE OF MY FAMILY)

CLOVER ED BE
WICHITA
Sedg. Co. Extension Service
9000 W. Central
722-7721

MY PET'S PAW
MY PET IS ☐ REAL ☐ IMAGINARY

MY FAMILY AUTOGRAPHS

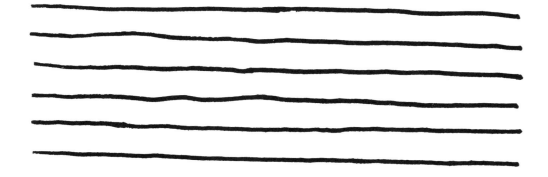

CLOVER CLUB WICHITA

Sedg. Co. Extension Service
9000 W. Central
722-7721

MY ROOM

I SHARE IT WITH:
___ PEOPLE   ☐ NO ONE
☐ A DOG   ☐ A CAT

THE WALL COLOR IS: _____.
IT HAS ___ WINDOWS
AND ___ BED(S).
THERE ARE ___
CLOSETS.
IT IS ___
STEPS FROM
MY BED TO
THE
DOOR.

MY HOUSE

IS IN: ☐ THE COUNTRY ☐ TOWN
       ☐ THE SUBURBS

MY HOUSE IS IN THE
TOWN OF _____

ON THE PLANET
_____

Clover Clubs

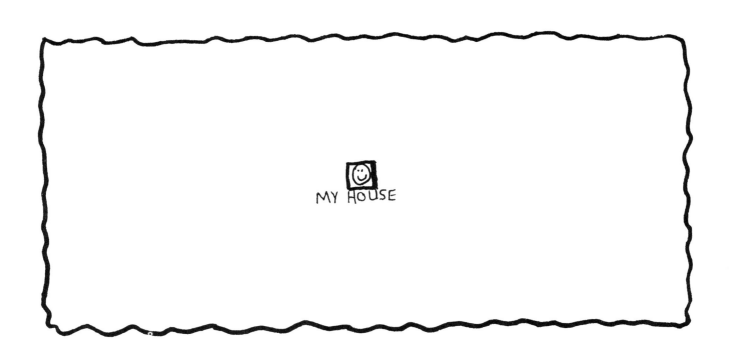

MY HOUSE

MY NEIGHBORHOOD MAP

(TRY USING COLORED PENCILS ON THIS)

I DREW IN:

- ☐ NEIGHBORS HOUSES
- ☐ ROADS
- ☐ STORES
- ☐ BUILDINGS
- ☐ ANIMALS I SEE ALL THE TIME
- ☐ PLACES I LIKE TO GO

- ☐ MAILBOXES
- ☐ TREES
- ☐ FLOWER BEDS
- ☐ VACANT LOTS

I DREW IN _____ LIVING THINGS (HOW MANY?)

I DREW IN _____ NON-LIVING THINGS.

CLOVER CLUB WICHITA

Sedg. Co. Extension Service
9000 W. Central
722-7721

MY TOWN AUTOGRAPHS
(MOST KIDS CAN'T GET THEM ALL)

OUR MAILMAN _____

A GROCER _____

A FIREMAN _____

A DELIVERY PERSON _____

A TELEPHONE OPERATOR _____

OUR GARBAGE COLLECTOR _____

A POLICE OFFICER _____

A JUDGE _____

A LIBRARIAN _____

SOMEONE OVER 6' TALL _____

A CLERGYMAN _____

A DOCTOR _____

A LAWYER _____

A NEWSPAPER PERSON _____

A RETIRED PERSON _____

A FAVORITE NEIGHBOR _____

FRIENDS

MY BEST FRIEND'S NAME IS _____
MY BEST FRIEND IS A ☐ GIRL ☐ BOY ☐ DOG ☐ FISH
                    ☐ HORSE ☐ COW ☐ CAT ☐ BIRD

MY FAVORITE TEACHER IS _____
MY FAVORITE NEIGHBOR IS _____

I LIKE TO TALK TO PEOPLE ☐ YES ☐ NO

SPORTS

MY FAVORITE SPORT TO WATCH IS _____
MY FAVORITE SPORT TO PLAY IS _____
I'M ☐ GOOD   ☐ O.K.   ☐ NOT SO GOOD

WORKING

THERE ARE ____ MEMBERS OF OUR FAMILY

____ WORK AT HOME

____ WORK AWAY FROM HOME

____ GO TO SCHOOL

ONE DAY, I WENT ALONG WITH A FAMILY MEMBER TO HIS/HER JOB. THE FAMILY MEMBER IS MY

_____

WHO WORKS AS A _____

AT_____

HE/SHE EXPLAINED A LOT OF THINGS ABOUT HIS/HER WORK. HERE ARE SOME THINGS HE/SHE DOES ON THE JOB._____

_____

_____

I THINK I'D LIKE A JOB LIKE HIS/HERS

☐ YES   ☐ NO

HERE'S WHY _____

_____

CLOVER CLUB WICHITA

Sedg. Co. Extension Service
9000 W. Central
722-7721

CHAPTER 3

Self-Reinforcement As Stress Management

INTRODUCTION OF CONCEPT

Stress management requires the belief that WE CAN CHANGE! It is possible to reinforce and strengthen ourselves toward initiating and increasing desired behaviors. We can take action to influence our own behaviors.

1. Self-Affirmation

A self-affirmation is a statement of positive decision. Self affirmations give confidence to the speaker to believe his own words can perhaps change his environment. The act of thinking or verbalizing these affirmations creates a movement toward their occurrence. Examples of such affirmations are:

I am a valuable person.

I desire life; I desire health, I desire love.

I am accomplishing my life goals.

I can relate positively to the people I love and care for.

All things are working for good.

2. Self-Rehearsal

Self-rehearsals are positive statements a person may repeat when anticipating a challenging or risky situation. They can be repeated under both stress and non-stress conditions to increase confidence and self encouragement. It is useful to state such rehearsals in positive rather than negative words. A negative self-rehearsal, "I will not get sick", may promote the feeling that I am in fact afraid of becoming sick. "I am healthy" is a more effective self-rehearsal.

One useful sequence of self-rehearsal is:

I want to   (be strong).

(e.g. learn to swim, be healthy, attractive, or intelligent)

I can   (be strong).

I am going to   (be strong).

I am   (becoming strong).

(e.g. learning to swim, being healthy, attractive, or intelligent)

3. Visualizations

Visualizations are the mental pictures, sounds, fantasies, and even feelings that we experience every day about the world in which we live. Our internal imaginations may center on past of futures scenes, and we often talk to ourselves inside (self-talk). Whatever we strongly expect, and what we choose to visualize, fantasize, imagine or say to ourselves, we tend to live out. All of our mental thoughts and visualizations affect the course of our living. This happens through the impact of repeated attention and the resulting inner programming. As a result it is very important to give attention to the quality and nature of our self-talk, imagination, and visualization. Negative hurtful expectations or visualizations promote negative, hurtful states of being and events ("I just know something awful is going to happen."). It is thus very important to create positive expectations and visualizations. These mental pictures, self-talk, and feelings in the camera of our mind can even become self-fulfilling prophesies, played out in our actual behavior patterns. The clearer and more detailed the visualization as we see ourselves, the more potent its effects, either positive or negative. Hearing the sounds, smelling the scents, imagining the sensory feelings, picturing the sights and experiencing the emotions all add strength to the mental representation of an event or state of being. The visualization is an extension of person "expectation" which exerts a profound effect upon what actually does take place.

We can learn to visualize good for ourselves and others. We can also help the children around us look for and concentrate on their positive hopes and desires.

Children can learn to imagine easily, but they may need assistance in turning their imaginations toward positive outcomes. Encouragement is a strong facilitating tool for helping them, e.g. "I'm glad that you...; I like it when you...; I think you are doing a good job in..."

Visualization, imagination, fantasy, self-talk, and all other internal mental processes can become very strong tools for personal growth. Some youth and adults are already adept at fantasy and fun imagination. Using how we "see" and "talk" to ourselves can become a major source of positive strength and confidence if our imagination and self-talk are purposefully positive.

One possible starter for a visualization is: Close your eyes, Relax and Think of the nicest thing that could happen in your life and imagine just how it would be; see how it looks; listen to the sounds; smell the smells; and touch what would be around you...

Another visualization might be: Close your eyes; Relax and Imagine yourself in a place where you are being criticized. See yourself respond to the person criticizing you with confidence, not angry or aggressive, just very firm in your own belief. Now, see yourself look for a solution that might please the other person but not give up your most important beliefs.

Another starter might be: Close your eyes, Relax, and Imagine yourself at a beautiful beach with acres of white sand and blue sky with a few puffy white clouds. The temperature is about 80 degrees or warmer and you feel just great. You can smell the ocean salt in the air, feel the moist spray of light waves, and hear the water lapping at the shore. Feel the warmth, peace, and calm of the beautiful day. Allow yourself to completely take in the relaxation, warmth, and calm of the setting.

As you see and feel yourself respond, you will feel more confidence in your ability to actually be firm, confident, and at peace even when attacked. Remember, if you cannot imagine (visualize) it; you cannot do it!

Finally, a quieting response to tension can be added by internal peaceful visualization such as the beach and calm self-talk. Just take a few minutes (two or three), take four or five deep breaths (to charge your body with fresh air), put your mind's eye on a mini-vacation to a pleasant place, tell yourself that you "are doing your very best", and finally, as you come back to the present, *smile* to yourself and others. That will quiet your inner

sense of self and prepare you for the next challenge of the day.

These concepts in action help create positive relationships by enabling positive self-respect in children, youth, and adults.

INTRODUCTION TO PARTICIPANTS

1. Self-Affirmation

All of us like to talk with people some of the time. Talking about things is one way of letting other people know what we think and who we are. People talk to themselves too. Some call it thinking out loud, or internal self-talk. We can help ourselves by talking in positive ways to ourselves. For instance, when I say, "I am a good person and I am doing my best", that statement helps me feel good about myself; it helps to do better than I was doing before; it encourages me. If I say "I'm so dumb, I always do the wrong thing", I am discouraging myself and making it harder for me to do better the next time.

2. Self-Rehearsal

How we talk to ourselves is very important because when we tell ourselves bad things, we are likely to mess up, but the more we tell ourselves good things, the more we are able to do better than before.

What kinds of things do you say to yourself? Do you say encouraging things or do you say discouraging things?

(ENCOURAGE DISCUSSION)

Think for a moment what you would especially like to be or do today. Make up a sentence to encourage yourself by saying, "I am doing a good job in (spelling); I am doing my best in (spelling); I am doing well in (spelling)." If you were to say this a few times to yourself as you study (spelling), your (spelling) will be better than if you had not encouraged yourself, or if you had worried a lot. If you wonder whether you are an OK person, give yourself an encourager statement like "God loves me, and I can love myself", or "I am valuable and important because I am me". When you talk to yourself like this, you help make better things come true, and you learn to *believe in yourself*.

(ENCOURAGE DISCUSSION)

When you are looking ahead toward something that seems scary, that you fear, or are worried about, use these starters below, and fill in the things you want to do or be.

I want to (do well on the spelling test).

I can (do well on the spelling test).

I'm going to (do well in spelling).

I am (doing well in spelling).

3. Visualization

In your imagination (you might call this the TV or movie screen of your mind) there are often pictures or sounds. Lots of people think that they cannot change what is "playing" in their thoughts at any given time. This is not true. We can change the channels in our mind's eye and make our own movies "run" whenever we choose. It is sometimes hard to get rid of pictures and sounds we do not want in our thoughts, but it is easier to *replace* those bad thoughts with pleasant encouraging pictures and sounds. It is like having your own video cassette recorder (VCR) on which you can run any program you want, at any time.

Practice seeing yourself being and doing the things you desire most. As you do this, you are mentally practicing for the real thing. Good things will become more and more likely to happen for you as you practice. Always think of yourself in good situations doing good things. Replace any bad or negative thoughts immediately with good ones. You can do good things for yourself and the people around you by imagining positive scenes (playing good movies) on your inner TV.

Remember, the power of positive (happy) thinking really is *powerful for you!* Build positive relationships by being positive (happy) to yourself.

INTERACTION ACTIVITIES

What Can I Do

Begin a discussion of self reinforcements by having each person list ten things he can do. Be ready to offer suggestions if he has trouble remembering his skills. Discuss how he learned those tasks, and encourage him to use his self-reinforcements when learning new behaviors.

I Can

Encourage persons involved in activities to verbalize "I can complete this task". Manual skills just within the ability range of the participants work well for this kind of affirmation.

Experiencing The Goal

Demonstrate how to do a task such as bouncing and catching a ball. Let the persons in the group try the task as a group, and then give them an opportunity to practice in pairs. Group together a person who completed the task well and one who needed more practice. After a few minutes of practice, bring them back to the circle and try the task again as a group. Encourage them to realize their progress. Discuss self-reinforcements. Now try the same process again with a new task, this time encouraging persons to use verbal self-reinforcements. Do you notice any difference in the amount of time it takes to learn the skill? Discuss the difference self-reinforcement makes.

Self Contracts

Ask each person to think of an area in his life which he would like to be different. Have him write a contract on how he will change that behavior in the next week. Encourage realistic and attainable steps toward the goals. Have volunteers discuss their contracts if appropriate. Instruct them to sign their names and take their contracts home as reminders. Be sure to follow up the next week by giving the persons a chance to share about their experiences with changing behaviors. Reinforce participants for all efforts.

Self-Reinforcement—Letters To Myself

Encourage persons to write self-rehearsals or affirmations related to things they want to change in their lives. Provide some structure to help persons begin writing. For example, post the openers "I want to..."; "I can..."; "I'm going to..."; "I am...". Use a game technique such as spinning a spinner, throwing dice, or drawing numbers to facilitate sharing.

Peak Sensations

Discuss each person's favorite things to see, touch, smell, taste, and hear. Have them write down one favorite category. Discuss possible ways they could treat themselves to a favorite sense when they want to reinforce or reward themselves. Emphasize that rewarding ourselves is useful because we may work better when looking forward to our self-provided "reward".

Next Week

Talk about new or frightening experiences each person in the group may be expecting next week. Plan how to use self-reinforcements to help in meeting the challenges. Frame and practice them in dyads or within the full group. Active listen to any emotion, such as fear or dread; then invite the participant to frame his own positive self-rehearsal in words or visualizations.

What I Want To Happen

Have persons draw, form in clay, cut out, or act out what they want to have happen in the future (tomorrow, next week, next year, or whenever). Discuss ways of moving toward the goals.

Variation: Use one of the above media to answer the question "What do I want to be like in the future?" Discussion can emphasize and clarify the importance of self-reinforcements in helping these future events occur.

New Behaviors Diary

Invite participants to keep a diary for one week of the new behaviors they attempted that week. Give them the New Behaviors Diary poster (see end of chapter), have them decide on a goal behavior, fill it in on the poster and take the poster home to help keep a record of progress. As they write down the new activities they tried, they can also record how successful they felt in attempting the new activity. This will help them learn to recognize and believe in their own abilities to try new behaviors.

Around The World Visualizations

Verbally direct the group on a trip to a different country. Use images characteristic to that culture such as describing whether it is hot or cold, what the terrain is like, what plants are growing, etc. Let persons walk around the room imagining they are in those situations, and responding however they desire and believe to be appropriate. Encourage follow-up study of other cultures and places. This exercise can broaden horizons and interests and carries within it some self-reinforcing experiences. Encourage participants to verbalize these.

Visualization Practice

1. Invite participants to form a circle, sit down, close their eyes and visualize one scene from the last week of their lives which was not a pleasant experience for them. Instruct them to imagine how that situation could have been better, and to visualize every aspect of a new scene. Encourage them to "run a mental movie" of how they would like the event to have occurred. Take time for each person to share.

2. Next, ask them to imagine a situation which they think might occur in the week ahead. Again, instruct them to visualize every detail of the situation happening as they hope it will. Encourage them to imagine smelling the smells, seeing the scenes, and hearing the sounds which might be associated with the desired occurrence of the situation. Take time for discussion and for each person to share.

I Can And I Am!

Divide the participants into small groups. As leader, share with the group something you can now do but which you previously feared to try (e.g. swimming, skiing, speaking before a group, etc.). Next, invite group members to think of something they have learned to do which was previously fearful to them. Invite them to share about how they learned, where they gained courage to try, and how they feel about these things. Encourage each to share, and discuss to promote thinking toward further positive change.

Variation: invite each participant to frame a self-reinforcer for the skill or achievement he has already learned. Then invite each to think of something he would *like* to be able to do but has not tried. Assist each to frame a self-reinforcer to prepare for trying to master that skill or achievement.

Use the following format or one which is similar:

I want to... (learn to ride a bike, improve my spelling, ask for a date, etc.)

I can... (same as above)

I'm going to... (same as above)

I am... (same as above)

Encourage participants to practice their self-reinforcement or rehearsals. Use dyads to practice and then report back to the group. Deal with negative feelings by active listening. Do not give solutions, logic, or advice. If, however, the individual is having difficulty, assist him on a one-to-one basis.

✛ ✛ ✛ ✛

I Can Design My World

Invite the participants to sit in a circle, close their eyes and visualize themselves far above the world in a space ship looking down at planet Earth. Invite them to watch the forms of the continents as the planet rotates and gradually to bring themselves over the North American continent where they can see the shape of the United States. Note the Great Lakes, the Atlantic and Pacific Oceans and then look for the general area within which they live. Invite them to imagine themselves looking at their State, their City, and then their block and finally the roof of the building within which they live. Invite them to imagine they have X-ray vision and can see through the roof into the space which is theirs

in that building. Now, invite them to look carefully at each detail of that space. Is the area neat or messy? Are the colors what they would like? NOW! Invite them to design exactly what they would want by using the following narrative: Please imagine that you now have unlimited power and resources to change your space so that it will be exactly as you would like it. Look at the walls, the ceiling, the floor. Would you like to design them into a different shape, color? Please do so in your mind's eye. Furnish your space just as you would like it to be. Add anything you would like. A swimming pool? A trampoline? Just visualize how you would like it to be. Notice how the textures of your new floor coverings feel to your feet. Touch the furniture, the coverings, the door handles. Note the new smells. Has your space become larger? Smaller? Have you added some things? Taken away some things? Please walk around in your imagination and note every detail and when you are ready, come back to this room in your mind and open your eyes.

Allow each person time to share his imagery without criticism from anyone. Reinforce all openness and sharing. If the group is too large to do this in one segment, divide into smaller components and give ground rules for sharing (e.g. each person has time to speak, judgment is reserved by all so that no one feels put down, acceptance and variety are encouraged).

✛ ✛ ✛ ✛

The "I" Can (Group)

Materials: Paper
Coloring Materials
Glue
Scissors

Decorate can (approximate #10 in size) with "I's" of all shapes, sizes, and designs. Invite all participants to design their own "I's" decorated in their individual styles, initialed and glued to the "I" can.

Place slips of paper with performance tasks written into the "I" can. Let these either be prepared ahead by the leader or brainstormed and prepared by the group during the decorating of the can or after completion of the decorating. Each participant will draw a slip from the can, read the task, reinforce himself and then proceed with the task. He may also need reinforcement from the leader and others! (Let the tasks be possible for everyone but include a small element of social risk.)

Suggestions for tasks:

1. I can tell the group how I feel right now.

2. I can hold my breath for fifteen seconds.

3. I can ask for help from someone in this group.

4. I can stand up and walk around the group and shake hands with each member

5. I can read this poem to the group:

> If I really think I can
> Then I really can.
> If I think I maybe can't
> Then I simply shan't.
>
> It's as simple as can be
> I'm the one to choose
> Whether I will try and win
> Or whether I will lose.

6. I can rearrange the chairs in this room the way I would like them to be.

7. I can ask everyone in this group to join with me in singing "America".

8. I can build a tower of objects which are in this room including people if I choose to ask them to help me.

9. I can close my eyes and imagine that I am in another place and then tell the group where my mind's eye has taken me.

10. I can pretend that I am a great conductor and that every member of this group is playing an instrument in a great band. I can ask each member what instrument he would like to play and form a band or orchestra which then can perform the great "Silent Symphony" with me as conductor!

ARTS AND CRAFTS

"I Can" Pictures

Invite participants to draw pictures of things they can do now that they could not previously do. They could also draw a composite picture of many things they can do. Discuss the process of learning new skills. Help them to understand that positive self-talk is help-

ful ("I'm doing my best"; "I want to... I can... I'm going to... I am...").

Success At Tie Dyeing

Materials: Cloth
               Dye (use a brand that requires hot but not boiling water)
               Containers for Dye
               Newspapers
               Clothespins and line
               String or rubber bands

Have each person bring an article of old clothing or part of a sheet and instruct them to gather the fabric in bunches and wrap it with string or rubber bands. Show all persons how to dip these bunches of fabric into the dye solution. When the fabric has reached the color that is desired, take off the string or rubber bands. Hang items on clothesline to dry. Model the use of self-reinforcement during the steps of the activity to encourage persons to believe the final product will turn out well and the project a success.

God's Eyes

Materials: Varied colors and weights of yarn
               Sticks or dowels (about tinker toy medium size)

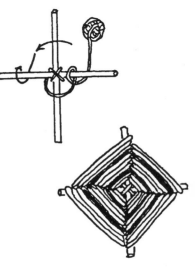

Help persons fasten together two sticks by wrapping them at the joint with string or yarn. At the center joint, they can loop the yarn over both arms several times to hold it securely. Next, have them wrap the yarn once around each arm, stretch to the next arm, and continue to wrap around one arm after the other. Vary the colors of yarn for an interesting and beautiful hanging ornament. Keep going until the ornament is the desired size. Talk about positive self-rehearsals as you tie the yarn, thinking of new self-rehearsals with each loop around the ornament. This is a never-fail activity with practically any age group.

✛ ✛ ✛ ✛

Turntable Trick

Materials: Record player (only the
turntable needs to function)
Circles of heavy paper
cut to the size of the turntable
Marking pens

Invite participants to take turns placing a circle of paper on the record player with the speed of 78 rpm. Instruct them to hold a marking pen on the revolving paper so that the movement of the turntable will produce an interesting pattern on the paper. Try using different colored pens, and visualizing how each will look. Self-rehearse about the beautiful designs each person will make. Encourage all efforts.

Variation: Use model paint instead. Let drops of paint fall on the paper as the turntable turns around.

✛ ✛ ✛ ✛

Printing With Objects

An important part of printing is attempting to visualize what the printed page will look like before it is actually printed. Have your group practice visualizing the results of the printing.

Gather a number of common objects such as toys with wheels, spoons, cups, and combs. Dip the objects into paint to cover the wheels, points or rims and print with them on paper. Compare the completed print with the group's visualization of how it would look.

✛ ✛ ✛ ✛

Graphics With Wood And String

Materials: Wooden blocks
one to three inches square
String
Glue
Paper
Tempera paints
Brushes
(common art paint brushes)

Invite each participant to coat the entire length of his string lightly with glue and then to wrap the string

around the wooden block to form a design that pleases him. Invite him then to dip one side of the block into the tempera liquid paint and to press it on the paper (paint may also be applied to the string with a brush).

Encourage some "trial runs" till participants get the hang of it, using lots of protective covering such as plastic and newspaper both on them and on the exposed surfaces.

Encourage them to make whatever designs please them with the "printing presses" on the paper. Encourage all efforts and promote self-reinforcement.

✛ ✛ ✛ ✛

Sponge Printing

Give each participant a dry plastic sponge and invite him to draw or trace a design on it. He may then cut out the design shape, dip the sponge in paint, and print with it on paper. Encourage him to reinforce himself while carrying out the project and encourage all efforts toward creativity.

✛ ✛ ✛ ✛

Stringer Designs

Materials: String
Cardboard, soft wood, boards
or cork
Paper
Chalk, varied colors
Thumb tacks
Plastic spray or fixatif

Invite participants to press a thumb tack into a board or cardboard and then to tie a string to the tack. Rub colored chalk on the string, place paper under the string against the board, pull the string taut and snap the chalked string against the paper. The chalk will transfer onto the paper in interesting designs. Try various colors, locations on the paper, and combinations. Lines may be blurred by stroking, and the shapes can be outline as desired to form patterns and pictures.

Encourage the participants to self-rehearse positive statements as they create their designs.

Fix the chalk to the paper with a protective coating of clear plastic spray or fixatif.

✛ ✛ ✛ ✛

Whirlie-Swirlie Art

Materials: Powder or oil paint
Shallow tray with water
Small mixing bowls
Paper
Turpentine
Soap
Paper Towels

Pour a small amount of the turpentine into one of the small mixing bowls and add enough paint to bring the mixture to the color desired. Pour the colored turpentine onto the surface of the water in the shallow tray and stir the water. The turpentine will cause the paint to form interesting patterns. Invite participants to carefully drag paper across the surface of the water and note how the color is picked up. Various colors may be used and experimentation with dragging and coloration can be encouraged. Invite participants to reinforce themselves as they create their unique pictures. Suggest that they visualize how the picture will look by observing the surface of the water before introducing the paper to the mixture.

✢ ✢ ✢ ✢

Paper Fantasies

Materials: Thin paper
Scissors
Rubber cement
Heavier colored paper

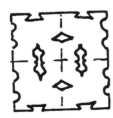

Invite participants to fold the paper into small square or oblong shapes. Cut numerous small designs from the folded paper until there is more paper cut away than remaining. Try to visualize how the design will look when the paper is unfolded. Unfold the paper and note the interesting design. The design can then be attached to contrasting colored paper, forming a see-through effect.

✢ ✢ ✢ ✢

I Want To... I Can... Collages

Materials: Paper or tag board for base
Magazines with many pictures
Scissors
Glue
Plenty of space to work

Invite the participants to look through magazines for pictures of activities or situations which they would like to experience (select magazines which will offer a variety of worthwhile and interesting materials for them to use). Encourage them to creatively put together a collage of these pictures gluing them to the base paper but leaving space for self-reinforcement or rehearsal to be lettered in. Assist them in affirming their own desires and lettering in as many parts of the rehearsal formula as they wish. Participate as leader by creating your own collage and modeling the type of creativity you wish to see in the other participants. (Formula: I want to... I can... I'm going... I am!)

✢ ✢ ✢ ✢

Toothpick Sculpturing Or Architectural Affirmations

Materials: Toothpicks (a lot)
Glue (white)
Paper or other material for base
Jar lid or something similar
on which to place individual
working amount of glue.

Invite participants to make their own toothpick creations by attaching toothpicks together with white glue. This requires a little patience, for the glue must dry somewhat before it will sustain weight. Most age levels above six can work with this, however. Encourage them to create a structure of sculpture which portrays something they want to see, do, or otherwise experience. Some like to build towers, others mountains, others free forms. Whatever they create is worthy and can be affirmed and reinforced. Encourage them to reinforce themselves as they work. Give completed structures time to dry; meanwhile, participants can each share their feelings and thoughts about their creations. If appropriate, invite the group to help each person name his creation.

The "I" Can (Individuals)

Materials: Paper
Colors of various types
including crayons, markers,
paint, etc.
Glue
Scissors

Invite each individual to decorate his own personal "I" can (soup size or just larger) with "I" symbols of various types and his initials. Let them make real productions of their cans (these can serve as pencil holders at home when the activities are over).

Invite each participant to write on a piece of paper a list of things he or she would like to do during the week which are personal goals. Explain the self-reinforcement idea, and assist them in framing their statements so as to be self-encouraging (e.g. I can make my bed each day; I can remember to put my bike away after I use it: I can...). Encourage each individual to frame his own real desires and goals.

Use the "I" cans for a take-home to serve as reminders of the goals which have been set. Make sure the participant has the "magic formula"—I want to, I can, I'm going to, I am.

INDIVIDUAL CENTERS

Changing My Attitude

My mother said I could not go,
Your mother said you could.
You didn't want to play the game,
I said I really would.

I had to walk to school today,
My sister got a ride.
My friends went to the park to play,
I had to stay inside.

My teacher said I talked in school,
I didn't say a thing.
The class all laughed at music time,
I didn't get to sing.

I told my friend I liked him,
He said he didn't care.
I shook my head and told myself,
I think that it's not fair.

But feeling sorry for myself
Won't help this awful mood.
So if I want to change my day,
I'll change my attitude.

To change my attitude I will
Identify the names
Of all the things I fell inside
My sadness, joy or shame.

Another way I'll change is just
To talk with those who'll hear
My mom or dad or friends of mine
Will help me learn to share.

In fact I'll try to influence
The folks I see each day,
To share their feelings openly
And learn from this new way.

1. Make a list of the attitudes and feelings you'd like to change in yourself.

2. Draw or cut out pictures of how you would like to do this.

I Can

I can do a lot of things
When I think I can.
If I reinforce myself,
I'll complete my plan.

I can give a message clear
Straight from me to you.
I can tell you how I feel,
You can tell me too.

If I start my messages
Clearly with an "I"
Then I know you'll understand
Who and how and why.

Congratulations

Let an individual fill in his name on this poster (see end of chapter) to create a certificate affirming that he is a winner. Invite him to decorate it as he desires.

Others Think I Am Special Too!

This poster provides space for the person to fill in names of other people who think he is special (see posters at end of chapter). Let him decorate the poster, and help him brainstorm if he has trouble thinking of people who value him.

+ + + +

I Am Something Special

Provide art materials so a person can draw a picture of himself on the poster (see end of chapter) and decorate it. It is an affirmation for that person to remind him that he is special.

+ + + +

Winners See What They Want To Be

This poster asks questions about what the person does well now, and what he would like to do well (see end of chapter). "Winners See What They Want To Be" poster can help

him realize what he does well now and help him identify areas that need to improve.

+ + + +

This Is A Recording

Provide a tape recorder and blank tape for an individual to record privately his self-reinforcements. Let him share them in the way he desires.

+ + + +

Group Graffiti

Post a large sheet of newsprint or butcher paper on the wall. Start some sentences but leave them unfinished for group members to complete such as: Today, I want to…; I hope you will…; I like…; When you…; I feel…; I am…; I believe…

Encourage persons to go to the graffiti wall and write however they desire. They may choose to complete the sentences or to let off steam by writing their own ideas of feelings.

BOOKS

Picture Books

Alexander, Martha G., **We Never Get To Do Anything.**
Aruego, Jose, **Look What I Can Do.**
Burton, Virginia Lee, **Katy And The Big Snow.**
Green, Mary M., **Is It Hard? Is It Easy?**
Hoban, Lillian Aberman, **Arthur's Honey Bear.**
Hurwitz, Johanna, **Superduper Teddy.**
Piper, W., **The Little Engine That Could.**

Fiction Books

Ames, Mildred, **Nicky And The Joyous Noise.**
Bunting, Anne Evelyn, **The Waiting Game.**
Gross, Alan, **What If The Teacher Calls On Me?**
Moore, Emily, **Something To Count On.**
Schick, Eleanor Grossman, **Joey On His Own.**
Smith, Doris Buchanan, **Last Was Lloyd.**
Udry, Janice May, **Mary Jo's Grandmother.**

Winners SEE what

they want to BE

WHAT I DO WELL NOW	WHAT I WOULD LIKE TO DO BETTER
1. AT HOME	
2. AT SCHOOL	
3. WITH FRIENDS	
4. WITH FAMILY	
5. ALONE	
READ YOUR LIST EVERY DAY FOR A WEEK.	IF YOU CAN DO THESE THINGS WELL, YOU CAN DO OTHER THINGS WELL.

I AM SOMETHING

SPECIAL

(DRAW A PICTURE OF YOURSELF)

Others think I am special, too!

These people think I'm special:

_____   _____

_____   _____

_____   _____

New
Behaviors
Diary

Name _____

Week of _____

Goal-this week I will try:

_____

_____

	Today for the first time I tried...	After trying this new behavior I felt.... because....
MONDAY		
TUESDAY		
WEDNESDAY		
THURSDAY		
FRIDAY		
SATURDAY		
SUNDAY		

Congratulations!

This award is to announce to the world that

_____

is an authorized winner who can proudly say,

"I'm glad I'm me!"

CHAPTER 4

Positive Reinforcement

INTRODUCTION OF CONCEPT

A reinforcement is a consequence liked to a behavior which increases the probability that the behavior will occur again. We are focusing on spoken or written positive reinforcements because they encourage good feelings in the receiver as the positive behavior associations are learned.

The most effective reinforcement is immediate, individual, and varied so that the receiver quickly feels noticed in a pleasing way. Positive reinforcement can be verbal or nonverbal and can be simple or part of a complex behavioral program.

Although children often feel powerless to change their situations, anyone can use positive reinforcement. This is one excellent tool which can help youth positively influence people in their lives (including adults). In this way they can make important changes in their social environments.

Some of the verbal positive reinforcers (encouragements) are:

I like it when you... (describe the behavior)

I think you are... (Something positive)

I'm glad that you...
(a desired behavior or condition)

I think it's great when you...
(desired behavior)

Thank you for...
(Statement of positive action or consequence)

The most effective encouragements or expressions of appreciations begins with "I". This is because a good pattern to follow for positive reinforcers is to own and claim each statement. To claim a statement begins with the word "I". This is an honest way to reinforcing without judging the person you are talking to.

Positive Reinforcement (verbal encouragement) is a powerful tool which gives positive attention while encouraging desirable behaviors. People around us will tend to repeat the behaviors we notice and comment on. "Catch them being good"[1] is a desirable goal to encourage and (positively reinforce) others. This positively impacts those around us, children, youth or adults.

Invite each participant to encourage and reinforce others by enjoying some of the activities which follow. In other words, teach the concept of encouragement by *demonstrating* it yourself to the youth you are working with. Invite them to encourage each other in practicing the process. Practice (rehearsal time) is by far the most effective way of teaching and acquiring a new functional skill in human relations. This tool (positive reinforcement, encouragement) is a strong component of relationship building.

INTRODUCTION TO PARTICIPANTS

A lot of people, perhaps you and I, tend to spend considerable time with our body-house doors and windows closed, thinking alone. When we try to talk to them and they do not seem to hear us or answer, it is pretty discouraging. We feel "shut out". Other people feel the same way about us when we do not pay attention to what they are trying to tell or show us.

A lot of people, perhaps you and I, spend time inside our body-houses with the doors and windows shut to other people. We need some time alone to rest and think, but when we knock on someone else's door (try to talk to them) and they don't seem to hear us or answer, it's discouraging. We feel "shut out". People feel the same way about us at times because we just are not tuned into what they are trying to tell or show us.

Perhaps you sometimes feel as if the people around you don't care very much about what you want or need or like. We call the gift, *"encouragement"* or a *"positive reinforcement"*. This is like taking a batch of freshly baked cookies and giving them to a friend for something they have done that you appreciate. The difference here is that the cookies are a gift of words.

The effects are a lot the same. People usually like positive reinforcements (encouragements). Most people are likely to do more of the things that bring them encouragement.

Here is an example of what we mean: Let's pretend that the cook prepared barbecued chicken for lunch today in the cafeteria. If you like barbecue chicken, you could tell the cook something like this:

> "I really like the chicken you fixed. Thank you for making it."

Next time the cook thinks about chicken, she will probably remember your kind words and be more likely to barbecue again. You gave the cook an encouragement, an expression of appreciation, a positive reinforcement. Another example would be if your mother or teacher wears a dress you like and you say to her,

> "I think that is a pretty dress and I like the way you look in it."

She is very likely to feel better about herself and be more likely to wear that dress again (She may also feel better about *you!*).

Another example is when you are having a problem (conflict) with a friend who did something unkind to you. Pick out some action you did like and tell that person how you appreciated that. For instance,

> "I really liked it when you helped me with my homework yesterday, thank you."

What happened was you said a very nice thing to your friend who had mistreated you. The friend may not respond positively at that time. You know, however, that you did not do an unkind thing yourself, and the friend may even respond better the next time to you.

This is a way to get people's attention in a pleasant way, it also helps make things better around you. Ignore the bad things in others as much as you can, but notice the good and tell people about the things you like in words. If you smile and look at the other person's eyes when you give encouragement, it is even better.

Discussion Questions:

What things have people done today that you would like for them to do more of?

Select a person to reinforce (encourage in words) and finish the following sentence:

"(Name), I like it when you _____"

or, "(I) thank you for _____."

INTERACTION ACTIVITIES

Animal Cracker Give Away Or Raisin Reinforcement

Ask each person in the group to practice giving positive reinforcements to other group members. To help them become more aware of the reinforcement process, provide them with some kind of  tokens to give away with their reinforcements. If the tokens are edible (such as animal crackers or raisins) ask persons *not* to eat their own tokens, but to eat those they receive from other people. This is an excellent activity for demonstrating positive reinforcements because everyone experiences how it feels to give and to receive reinforcements from each other.

Limbo Game

Have the group form a line and one by one go under the "limbo" stick. Each round, move the stick lower, so that it is more difficult to get under. Encourage the group to reinforce each other with statements such as: "I know you're going to make it", "I think you did a great job" or "I'm cheering for you".

Positive Reinforcement Through Games

Practice positive by having persons give reinforcements to each other while doing a skilled task as a group. Some activities that work well are obstacle courses, relay races, and group tangling and untangling games.

Time the group doing the task when positive reinforcement is not used. Then have them go through it again and really get in to reinforcing each other with statements like "I know you can do it", or "I think you're doing great". Compare the two times by stop watch or other measuring device to show how positive reinforcement increases group success. Encourage enthusiasm and cooperation.

+ + + +

What Do I Like?

Encourage each person to think of one thing she likes about each other person in the group. Discuss ways to reinforce those behaviors in others so they will happen more often. (See the "Zingers, Zonkers" poster at the end of the chapter for ideas).

+ + + +

Parcel Post Positive Reinforcement

Materials: Paper
             Pencil
             Postal exchange box

Invite each participant to prepare a simple "letter" for every other participant. Ask them to limit the letter to one positive reinforcement statement such as:

Dear Jason:

I felt good when you said "hi" to me. Thanks.

or

Dear Kari:

I think you have a nice smile.

Ask the participants to be specific and describe a behavior which they like and would like the receiver to do more often. Make the message person-specific. Claim the message by using the personal pronoun "I".

Some starters are:

I like it when you…

I'm glad that you…

I feel happy when you (or that you)…

I think you are…

Avoid the use of "It makes me" or "You make me".

Encourage the participants to sign their letters, but give them the option of leaving them unsigned. After the messages are written, invite the participants to place them in the mail box. Give time for all participants to receive their letters and read them. Then share around the circle for feedback and response by all recipients. Give them time to ask any questions as to what was meant by a message or to clarify and to express the feelings they experience during the activity.

Variation: This exercise can easily be adapted for various age levels. Simplify the letter writing or make it more complex according to the age and stage of the participants. Reinforce all efforts to cooperate.

+ + + +

I Can Encourage My Family

This is a "take-home" activity which requires some participation as follows:

Invite participants to write down the names of each of their family members on the handout sheets (end of chapter). Ask each participant to think of one thing they like about each family member or one behavior (action) they would like to see that person do more often. Explain that whenever they give a positive reinforcement to one of these persons they are doing two things:

1. Giving a valuable gift of esteem and appreciation.

2. Encouraging the person to do or be more of whatever they are reinforcing.

For example: If someone in my family says to me, "I think you look nice in those jeans", I am likely to wear those jeans more often. Or, if someone tells me, "I like it that you picked up the trash and emptied it", I am more likely to do it again. Or, if a member of my family says "I think this is good food. Thanks for fixing it", I will want to please them even more.

Encourage the participants to practice what they could say. Coach, model and reinforce them for all efforts.

Ask the participants to take the handout sheet home and make a check mark in the space provided each time they give a positive reinforcement to a person on the list including themselves. Be sure to share results the next week.

+ + + +

Reinforcement Stories

Read the following stories. Have participants act out the ending and think about the possibilities of positive reinforcement.

Bill always enjoyed going to the hardware store with his mother or dad, because he could look at all the fishing tackle and sports equipment. His dad would sometimes take him, and sometimes would go without saying anything. Bill had often begged his dad to go but that didn't seem to do anything except to get dad kind of grumpy at him.

One day dad said to Bill, "Want to go to the hardware store, Bill? I have some things to get there". What could Bill say or do that would make it more likely that dad would remember to take him other times later on. (Bill could say "Sure, I like to go to the store with you!" or "I'm glad you're taking me with you!")

Jane really loves eating fruit salad, but her mother doesn't fix it very often. Jane would be willing to help with the preparation, but when she offers to do that, mother doesn't seem too impressed. What can Jane do to make it more likely that her mother will prepare fruit salad? (Jane can give her a positive reinforcer the very next time she prepares fruit salad such as "I really like this salad, Mom!" or "I'm so glad you fixed fruit salad!")

Line Up For Friendship

Have the group brainstorm and compile a list of qualities which they think make a good friend. Write them horizontally across the board with space between the words, or decorate signs and hang them on the walls. Some starters are: willingness to spend time, honesty, caring, etc.

Ask persons to stand under the quality which best describes what they consider to be the most important aspect of friendship. Invite persons to share ways in which they are a good friend, and ways they would like to improve. Invite them also to share qualities of friendship which they feel other persons in the group demonstrate. Encourage full participation.[2]

Bombardment Game

Take a large stack of newspapers and spend some times tearing the sheets in half and wadding each half into a ball to create an "arsenal". Make a huge stack of balls, and then fire away, throwing as many paper balls as possible but with this one requirement: Each time an individual throws a paper ball, he must also say, yell, or otherwise communicate a positive reinforcement to the bombarded person. These can be quite free in form such as:

"I like it when you…"

"I like you…"

"I think you are…"

"I'm happy when you…"

Generate enthusiasm, spontaneity, and friendly exchange by modeling as leader.

Variation: Forget the paper and use imaginary snowballs. This is a winner too if the leader encourages free style fun and honest positive reinforcement expression.

Positive Reinforcement Skits

Divide into small groups and make up skits demonstrating how positive reinforcement works. Encourage the use of real life scenes in the skits.

Variation: Let some skits show what happens when positive reinforcement is not given and some when it is given to demonstrate the difference.

Role Play Reinforcements

Ask two group members to act out the situations and to give a positive reinforcer in response:

1. You have your arms full of books and packages which are slipping and falling. A friend takes some of them and relieves you by carrying them for you. (Give a positive reinforcement.)

2. You are walking in the rain and wanting to get someplace in a hurry. A friend stops and offers you a ride. (Give a positive reinforcement.)

3. You are cleaning up a mess the dog made. A member of your family brings a rag and some water and starts to help without being asked. (Give a positive reinforcement.)

4. You have fallen off your bike and are sitting in the road hurting and feeling badly. A friend helps you get up, checks your bike, and shows you she cares about you. (Give a positive reinforcement.)

5. You are getting angry and frustrated because a project you are doing, like sewing or cooking, or fixing the bike is not working. A member of your family offers to help you out. (Give positive reinforcement.)

Some examples of positive reinforcers are:

"I think its super when you…"

"I'm so glad that you…"

"I appreciate it when you…"

✛ ✛ ✛ ✛

What Will Happen If… ?

Invite each participant to think of some situation in her life which she would like to be different. Share around the group and select some which are typical and would lend themselves to change through positive reinforcement (e.g. competitive sports, school work, play situations).

Discuss and role play what realistically might happen in the various situations if positive reinforcement is given. This will be important in helping persons develop accurate expectations of how their positive reinforcement might be received.

ARTS AND CRAFTS

Reinforcement Collages

Discuss positive reinforcements and ask each person to make a list of all the people in her life who she could positively reinforce. Let her find pictures in magazines to represent each person on the list. She may then paste the pictures on a large sheet of paper, writing a positive reinforcement which each one such as "I like the way you share your books with me", or "I like it when you sing". Be sure to reinforce each person's collage ("I think you did a good job!" or "I'm glad you found those pictures.") Some persons will have fewer people to reinforce then others, so encourage them to think of more reinforcements that they may use for each one. This activity provides a practice experience which builds confidence for the person-to-person exchange.

✛ ✛ ✛ ✛

Group Mural

Materials: Newsprint
Tape
Scissors and glue
(if collage is to be made)
Paints, crayons, magic markers
or picture supply

Tape a length of newsprint to the wall with space for each participant to work. With all contributing, create a group mural on the theme "What I Do Best", "What I Think You Do Well", "What I Like About…"

Variation: Make a group collage using similar themes. Provide burlap, yarn, and large needles to sew a stitchery design to illustrate the themes (an ongoing group activity).

✛ ✛ ✛ ✛

Group Giveaways

Have persons make simple objects such as painted rocks, decorated walnuts or fuzzy balls with eyes. They may then give these away with verbal positive reinforcements such as "I like the way you smile at me", or "I like it when you…"

Variation: Have each person list on a sheet of paper some things she does well or likes in herself. Then provide tape for each participant to attach her list to herself in plain sight. Everyone then walks around and exchanges positive reinforcers based on what is written on the other person's sheet (e.g. "I think it's neat that you…")

✛ ✛ ✛ ✛

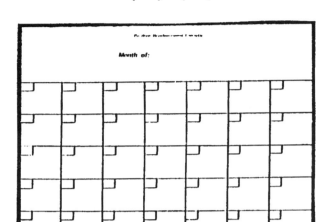

Positive Reinforcement Calendars

Let persons seasonally decorate the Positive Reinforcement Calendar Posters (see end of chapter) and fill in days of the current month in the spaces provided. Give them gummed stars or stickers, and instruct them to take the calendars home and glue a sticker on for each positive reinforcement they give each day. Discuss positive reinforcement and encourage them to think of people in their lives they would like to reinforce. Be sure to have them bring the calendars back at the end of the month and tell about their positive reinforcements.

Variation: When decorating the calendars, decide on special days when all persons in the group will reinforce their mothers, teachers, sisters, etc. They will write the person's name on the calendar for that day and report back to the group how the reinforced person responded.

✛ ✛ ✛ ✛

Family Maps

Materials: Paper
                 Pencil with erasers
                 Coloring materials

Make a "map" of your family by drawing circle for each member who lives together. Put yourself somewhere in the middle and make the other circles near or far from you and big or little compared to you to represent how you view these persons.

As leader, do a full demonstration telling why you are making some circles larger, others smaller, and why you are positioning them as you are. Speak also of which ones you would like to have nearer to you and larger or smaller. Be self-disclosing and open to the participants.

Invite participants to prepare their own family "maps", placing initials inside the circles to designate individuals. Provide coloring materials for another dimension and note choices of colors for later discussion.

When all have finished, encourage everyone to share who is near, who is far, big and little, and how they would like to have it different. Ask about color choices with acceptance and encouragement.

If the group is receptive, help them design positive reinforcements for each person or for those they want to reinforce. Give each participant space and do not be concerned if some are not ready to take this step. This exercise is thought-provoking and may elicit feelings. Be prepared to active listen when this occurs.

✛ ✛ ✛ ✛

Pictures In My Mind

Materials: Drawing materials

Take the group on a guided imagery as follows, or design your own. (Use soft voice and pause often to give time for participants to catch up.)

"Please close your eyes and imagine that you are in

your favorite place. Look at the sights, listen to the sounds, smell the fragrances, touch what you want to, and notice what is under your feet. Just be there for a few moments and enjoy everything you like about this place. Now imagine that you are walking along in your place, everything is as you like it, and down the way you see the form of a person and know that someone is there. As you get closer, you see that it is someone whom you like and enjoy spending time with. Think of some of the things you especially like about that person, and prepare to greet the person as you come closer. Now, when you are at speaking distance, greet this special person in a special way such as 'I am glad to see you here' or 'I think you are…' and fill in whatever fits for that person. Imagine that your special person responds to you, and listen to what is said. When you are ready, slowly return back the way you came. Look once more at the beauty of your place. Take your time and when you are ready, open your eyes and be here.

Now please take your paper and drawing materials and make any designs, pictures, or symbols which reflect what you saw and did in your mind. Use color if you like; be free to represent what you did any way you like on paper."

Invite participants to share their representations, but do not urge if any seem reluctant. Model positive reinforcement by giving it to them, and encourage them to reinforce one another.

My Salt Sculpture

Materials: A glass container with a top
A box of salt
Colored chalk, variety of colors
A spoon
Plastic lids or saucers
   for each color
A paper cup for each color

This art form will emerge by placing layer after layer of colored or plain salt in the glass jar. Each participant is to give a positive reinforcement to someone in the group before she pours each layer of his sculpture. The leader can model with a statement such as: "Joe, this first layer is for you, and I'm making it blue because I like the way your blue eyes twinkle when you smile." Or "Jean, this second layer is for you; it's red, and that's because red is a bright and happy

color for me and I like the way you are usually bright and happy". The activity can be simplified by ignoring the relationship of color to the individual and just giving a simple reinforcement while adding the layer.

Instructions for preparing the creating the sculpture:

1. Place two or three teaspoons of salt on a plastic lid or saucer, rub chalk over and over the salt until the salt is colored. Rub longer for deeper colors. Create as many colors as desired.

2. Place the colored salt into a paper cup until ready for use.

3. Gently pour one layer of color at a time into the glass jar, giving a reinforcement to someone in the group with each color.

4. Let the layers be as thick or as thin as you like them to be. The salt will fall unevenly and you can guide it into mounds as you like.

5. Fill the jar full; allow it to stand overnight to settle, then add more salt, put on the lid, and seal by screwing on the lid tightly.

This really makes a fun activity and an attractive sculpture. The amounts of salt, chalk, etc. will vary greatly according to the number of participants and the sizes of their jars. These can be gift wrapped with originally designed paper as special occasion gifts.

Reinforcement Rainbows Plus

Materials: An old sheet, preferably white
Scissors, glue, pencils
Needles and thread
Scraps of fabric in various
   patterns, textures and colors

Invite the participants to talk together about rainbows they have seen, their feelings when they see a rainbow, the colors in a rainbow, how it occurs in natural life, etc. Suggest that "making a rainbow" will be linked into giving each other the gifts of positive reinforcements of R+ (Rainbows plus).

Spread out the sheet or attach it to a wall space and draw six arcs making each wide enough so a large area of the sheet is utilized. Then cut away the cloth which will not be used for the rainbow. Mark each arc for its rainbow color (red, orange, yellow, green, blue, violet) to help remember the colors as participants work.

Cut or tear patches of fabric of each color which can be prints, solids, plaids, polka dots, or whatever. The shapes can be varied too. Glue the red patches on the first stripe, arranging them so that different fabric textures can be mixed. ONE REQUIREMENT! Before anyone glues on a patch, she is to give a positive reinforcement (R+) to someone in the group. The form can be very simple such as "I like to work with you", "I think you have a nice smile", "I appreciate your loaning me the glue" etc.

Work along on the various rainbow colors as time allows. This makes a good activity for early-comers or as a wind-down. It can be extended over several meeting times. Rainbow reinforcement teams can work on separate stripes.

INDIVIDUAL CENTERS

Say Something Positive

This poster (see end of chapter) asks the person to try to say something encouraging to everyone in her family, and then to record responses. The poster can be illustrated if desired.[3]

+ + + +

Zingers, Zonkers

Pass out the Zingers, Zonkers sheet (see end of chapter) and let persons fill in their positive reinforcements and negative statements. Discuss how reinforcements can be used to change situations.

+ + + +

Reinforcement Solitaire

Provide a flat space and a deck of cards with the two through tens removed from each suit. Let the player decide who each kind of card will represent such as:

> Aces = myself
>
> Kings = teacher
>
> Queens = mom
>
> Jacks = friend

Instruct the player to lay out eight cards face up in a line, then eight cards upside down on the top of the first cards. She can pick one of the eight piles and turn the top card over. The player must then make a positive reinforcement which the person represented by the top card could say to the person represented by the bottom card. For instance, if it happened to be a Queen over a Jack, the player would think up a reinforcement that her mom could give to her friend such as "I like the way you are playing today". If a pair of the same card turns up such as two Kings, the player would then think of a positive reinforcement which the teacher could say to herself. The player may do as many of the pairs as she desires.

BOOKS

Picture Books

Buckley, Helen Elizabeth, **The Wonderful Little Boy**.
Cohen, Miriam, **So What?**
Delton, Judy, **I Never Win**.
De Paola, Thomas Anthony, **Oliver Button Is A Sissy**.
Stanek, Muriel Novella, **Growl When You Say R**.

Fiction Books

Barrett, John M., **Daniel Discovers Daniel**.
Blume, Judy, **The One In The Middle Is The Green Kangaroo**.
Cohen, Miriam, **No Good In Art**.
Conford, Ellen, **The Revenge Of The Incredible Dr. Rancid And His Youthful Assistant, Jeffrey**.
Ets, Marie Hall, **Bad Boy, Good Boy**.
Gilson, Jamie, **Do Bananas Chew Gum**.
Hogan, Paula, **Sometimes I Don't Like School**.
Litchfield, Ada Bassett, **Words In Our Hands**.
Stolz, Mary Slattery, **The Bully Of Barkham Street**.
Udry, Janice May, **What Mary Jo Shared**.

Footnotes

[1] Wesley Becker, in Little People, Edward R. Christophersen, (Austin, Texas: Pro-ed, 1982), p. 7

[2] Joyce King and Carol Katzman, Imagine That (Santa Monica California: Goodyear Publishing Co., 1976), p. 126.

[3] Clover Club Wichita (Wichita, Kansas: Sedgwick County Extension Service), p. 14.

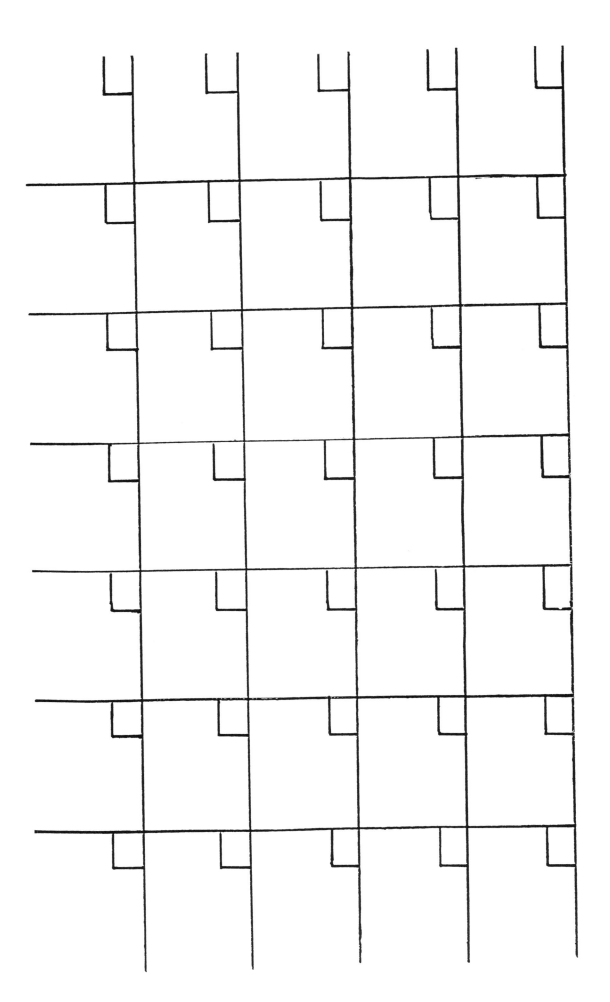

Positive Reinforcement Calendar

Month of:

SAY SOMETHING

TELL EVERYONE IN YOUR FAMILY SOMETHING NICE
ABOUT THEM BE HONEST. DO IT NOW.
WHAT HAPPENED? TELL ABOUT IT.
HOW DID YOU FEEL? _____
HOW DID THEY FEEL? _____
_____

NOW SIT DOWN WITH ONE FAMILY MEMBER
ASK HIM/HER TO SHARE WITH YOU THE THING
HE/SHE IS PROUDEST ABOUT IN HIM/HER SELF.
NOW YOU TELL WHAT YOU'RE PROUDEST OF IN
YOURSELF.
I TALKED WITH MY _____
HE/SHE IS PROUDEST ABOUT_____
I'M PROUDEST ABOUT MY _____

NOW ASK HIM/HER TO TELL YOU A STORY ABOUT
SOMETHING THAT HAPPENED TO HIM/HER THAT REALLY
FRIGHTED HIM/HER   WHAT DID HE/SHE DO?

NOW YOU TELL ONE ABOUT SOMETHING THAT FRIGATENED YOU.

Sedg. Co. Extension Service
9000 W. Central
722-7721

ZINGERS & ZONKERS

What you say to others paints pictures in their imagination and affects their feelings about themselves.

Zingers

MAKE PEOPLE FEEL GOOD!

HERE ARE SOME ZINGERS:

_____

_____

_____

_____

_____

_____

_____

_____

Zonkers

MAKE PEOPLE FEEL BAD!

HERE ARE SOME ZONKERS:

_____

_____

_____

_____

_____

_____

_____

_____

I Can Encourage My Family

Names of Family Members (Including Myself)	Monday	Tuesday	Wednesday	Thursday	Friday	Saturday	Sunday

CHAPTER 5

"I" Messages

INTRODUCTION OF CONCEPT

"I" Messages Used As Encouragers

In learning to take responsibility for our own behaviors, an area that we often overlook is the ownership (claiming) of our own verbal statements. This means that I take responsibility for what I think and state by using the pronoun "I" rather than the "you" which is so commonly heard.

"When *you* jog you feel better", is *not* claimed. The speaker lays the responsibility on "you".

"That's a pretty blouse" is *not* a claimed message and is thus a general statement which no apparent source. As a result, it has much less credibility.

"I like your blouse" is a claimed message. The speaker takes responsibility for the opinion, but does not make a judgment.

"I" messages that are positive, are very reinforcing (encouraging) to the person who receives them, as well as the person sending the message. They are also credible and more easily accepted by the receiver. "I think you did a great job" is a positive reinforcement. It does not make judgment, but instead states my opinion and gives encouragement. On the other hand, "You did a great job" (unclaimed) implies judgment and is more likely to be denied or forgotten by the receiver. The message simply has less positive impact.

"I" Messages Used To Confront

"I" messages are also useful non-blaming tools for confrontation. They work best when I desire the other person to change his behavior and when the relationship is strong enough to support confrontation. A confronting "I" message which is likely to influence the receiver to change behavior will have three components:

1. A non-blaming *description* of the receiver's behavior which is causing me a problem.

2. A statement of the sender's (my) *feelings*.

3. The *consequences* of the behavior to the sender (me).

For example: "When you walk into the house with mud on your feet (#1) "I" feel frustrated (#2) because I've cleaned and now it is dirty again" (#3)

This message offers the receiver a chance to be the "good guy" and change his behavior to help the sender. In contrast, a "you" message such as "You make me so mad!" is unclear concerning what the offending behavior is. This will have little effect except to anger or confuse the other person. A "you" message conveys a sense of judgment and will damage a relationship.

The "I" message, whether used to make a positive statement, *encouragement*, reinforcement, or is to *confront* another individual, is a useful and sometimes assertive tool for honest sharing and strengthening of human relationships.

INTRODUCTION TO PARTICIPANTS

As we listen to the ways people talk to each other, we can notice that the word "you" is used a great deal. People say things like, *"You* take your tennis racket, *you* hold it in your hand, and *you* throw the ball" when they are really talking about somebody else besides "you". Most often, they really mean themselves, but they hardly ever use just the simplest word which is "I".

We are going to think about "I" messages and practice them so that whenever we use the word "you" it will be because we really do mean YOU (the other person), and not because we are just saying the word.

An "I" message is a good way to say what I think or believe or feel or want. If another person is doing something which bothers, hurts or inconveniences me, I can tell him about it with an "I" message. This kind of "I" message has three parts.

First, I state *what* the behavior is that I want the other person to change. Then I tell him *my feelings* about it. Then I *explain what* it is doing to me.

Something like this:

"When you – – – (e.g. scratch your fingernails on the blackboard)".

"*I* feel – – – – – (e.g. nervous and edgy)".

"Because – – – – – (e.g. it hurts my ears)".

We can use the same way of speaking to tell someone about something they do which we like, and hope they will do more often. It works both ways.

"When you – – – (e.g. sharpen my pencils for me)".

"*I*" feel – – – – – (e.g. very pleased and happy)".

"Because – – – – – (e.g. they are ready to use when I need them)".

You can also reverse the order if you wish. For example:

"I feel (*happy*) when you (*smile at me*), because, then (*I know you like me*)".

This sample is using "I" messages as a positive reinforcement (encouragement). It is a very powerful type of reinforcement. Many people, especially parents and teachers, want to know and use the most powerful forms of encouragement. "I" messages are easy to understand and use since they usually start with "I" or have "I" as a main word in them.

Let's Practice Giving Some "I" Messages!

INTERACTION ACTIVITIES

"I"-Tag

Like freeze tag, one person is "it". When "it" tags another, the tagged person squats downward and is frozen until "saved" by getting eye contact on the same eye level, and an "I" message from a "free" person. If the game is slow, try having more than one person be "it". This is an active, fun way to practice "I" messages in a non-threatening situation. Coach players freely, and reinforce all efforts to participate.

"I" Can Say It

Invite participants to place themselves in two concentric circles which face an empty chair in the middle of the two circles. Open up a topic for discussion which is likely to be of interest to all. For example: "If you had $500.00 unexpectedly come your way, what would you do with it" or "What are you finding out about communicating with your family?"

The inner circle will discuss the selected topic. Participants in the outer circle may take part in the discussion only when someone in that circle chooses to sit in the chair in the center. In that case, he is entitled to make one "I" statement and is then to return to the outer circle. Only "I" statements may be from the empty chair, but anyone from the outer circle may move to the chair at any time or make an "I" statement as a part of the discussion.

The activity is designed to give practice and experience in framing "I" messages which express thoughts and feelings.

+ + + +

"It", "We", "You", And "I" Statements

To compare the differences between "I" statements and "it", "we", and "you" statements, divide the group into pairs and have them talk to each other in each of these ways:

1. Use only statements beginning with "it". Do not ask any questions, but attempt to carry on a discussion. Now talk about this experience. How did you feel as you made "it" statements and listened to those made by your partner?

2. Repeat the same procedure having all sentences beginning with "you".

3. Try it again with "we" statements.

4. Now, talk to each other using "I" statements. Compare this with the other experiences. In what ways were "I" statements easier to use? How where they harder?[1]

I Have To, I Choose To

Have persons in the group pair up and sit facing each other. Ask them to maintain eye contact and talk directly to each other through the activity. Now, instruct them to take turns saying sentences to each other that begin with the words "I have to…" and make a list of all the things they have to do.

When they are through with those sentences, have them go back to all the sentences and replace "I have to…" with "I choose to…", and take turns saying these new sentences. This activity helps persons realize they do have the power of choice, even if that choice is between two undesirable alternatives. Take a few minutes to discuss the activity. Did anyone have the experience of realizing his own responsibility for his choices? Did anyone discover any personal power from changing his pattern of speech?

Variations: Try the same exercise using the terms "I need" and substituting "I want". See if anyone experiences a sense of freedom in realizing that some needs are really only conveniences and not necessities.

Try once more replacing "I can't" with "I won't". Is there a feeling of strength in taking responsibility for refusals?[2]

✛ ✛ ✛ ✛

"I" Message Confrontations

Read the following situations one at a time and ask for members of the group to volunteer a non-blaming confronting "I" message which may influence the other person to change his behavior.

1. Your younger brother goes into your room when you are not there and moves your things around. Construct a confronting "I" message such as, "When you _____, I feel _____, because _____."

2. Your teacher makes long assignments and then forgets to ask for them to be turned in. Construct an "I" message such as, "When you _____, I feel _____, because _____."

3. A friend borrows your bike without asking and forgets to return it. Construct an "I" message such as, "When you _____, I feel _____, because _____."

✛ ✛ ✛ ✛

Alphabetical Feelings

Materials: Butcher paper and tape
                    to hold it to wall or board
                    Magic markers or equivalent

Write at the top of the paper "I feel _____ when…"

Under the blank, list the alphabet

A
B
C, etc.

Invite the participants to brainstorm for feelings which they have felt at different times which begin with each letter of the alphabet. If they cannot come up with one, go right on and come back to the missing letter. Give lots of leeway for feelings such as Awful, Bad, Corny, Dippy, Excited, Funny, etc.

When all the letters of the alphabet are completed with a feeling (except perhaps X, and your group genius may be able to help with that one), use one of the following processes or make up your own:

1. Invite the group to "group-tell" a story using the feelings (e.g. Once upon time Joe was feeling Awful because so many Bad, Corny things had been happening, and yet he was Excited too about… etc.) Go around the circle, giving each participant the opportunity to add or to pass. Give time so that the natural "brain-stormers" do not take over the exercise. All can usually participate.

2. Discuss some of the feelings, giving simple structure such as "When _____ happened, I felt _____". Invite each participate to select a feeling and complete the blanks in the sentence.

3. Consider the exercise finished for that time when the alphabet is fairly well completed. Keep it posted as a reminder, and use it another time if appropriate. Be sure to give the group time to talk about the exercise before leaving it. Some feelings will have been surfaced during the process of completing the list. Encourage sharing.

✛ ✛ ✛ ✛

"I" Message Letters

Materials: Paper
                    Crayons or markers
                    Large envelopes (legal size)

1. Before any other group activities, invite each participant to complete the following sentence in his mind: "Right now I feel _____", using only one word for the completion. When each has chosen his word, hand out paper and make crayons or markers available. Invite each person to write out

his claimed feeling word and to surround it with colors and designs which help him to express that feeling. Place each completed word design in an envelope, seal and have each participant sign his envelope. Keep envelopes together until ready for part #2.

2. At the end of your time with the group, invite each participant to again complete the sentence "Right now I feel _____" and create a design to express this feeling. Then hand back the first envelope and give time for participants to compare the first with the second.

3. Invite the participants to form a circle or to work in small groups for sharing their feeling comparisons. Encourage claimed "I" messages. Model by doing the exercise with the participants and sharing honest feelings in clear, claimed messages.

"Feedback For Me"

Materials: Heavy paper or tag board fashioned into a headband for each participant. Prepare a satisfactory way of fastening which will allow for head size differences.

On each headband, letter a message such as:

"Feel sorry for me"

"Treat me like royalty"

"Get me to give you some advice"

"Act as if I'm not here"

"Help me"

"Treat me like a joke"

"Disagree with me"

"Do whatever I say"

"Boss me around"

"Make me your leader"

"Treat me like a fragile flower"

Each participant is to have a headband placed on his head without his knowing what it says; however, everyone else in the group is to be able to read it.

Give the group a discussion subject of general interest, and instruct the participants to talk naturally, but to relate to the other participants in the manner indicated by their headbands. Request them not to tell one another what their headbands say. Topics might be: "What do you think about U.F.O.'s?" or "What is the best movie you've seen lately?"

When the activity has run its course so that everyone has experienced the impact of relating to and being related to in unfamiliar ways, invite each person to guess what is written on his headband.

Discuss as a group some of the experiences encountered during the exercise. Some lead questions are:

1. How did you feel when someone reacted to you in an unexpected way?

2. Did you change your manner of relating to others based on their behaviors toward you? (e.g. melt into the woodwork when treated as if not there).

3. Did you learn some things about how it feels to be misinterpreted?

4. Did you gain some sensitivity and insight about how others may feel?

Give the participants time so that each can share. Then discuss "I" messages as "straight talking" ways to convey feelings, needs, and ideas to others without attacking them. Point out the honesty of "I" messages and their use in conveying information between persons. Invite each participant to make one "I" statement to the group or to an individual concerning his experiences in the activity and sharing time.

I Am...

Seat participants in a circle. Warm up the group by role playing a phone conversation where the leader "calls" several group members, pretending that he does not know them, but will need to be able to recognize them in a crowd. In the "telephone conversation", ask the participant pertinent questions such as "How tall are you", "What color is your hair", "What are some distinguishing features by which I could recognized you?" After several have participated, give paper and pencil to each group member. Invite all to write a brief self-description using positive "I" messages (I am...). When everyone has had time to do this, collect the papers, and distribute them randomly so no one gets his own. Go around the circle having each person read the paragraph he holds aloud, and then have him guess who the writer is. If the reader cannot identify the writer, have the writer stand and identify himself. After each paragraph is read and the writer identified, the paper is to be returned to its writer. The purpose of the exercise is to give and receive information and feedback concerning self-appearance and concept. Encourage positive discussion with particular emphasis on positive "I" messages.

"I" Message Role Play

Have the players sit in a circle. The person who is "it" stands facing someone in the circle and states "I am your... (mother, father, sister, brother, coach, etc.) and I want to... (state whatever he wants such as 'Eat your spinach', 'Hang up your clothing', or 'Make lots of baskets')". That person then has until "it" counts to twenty to either pantomime what he was asked to do or give an "I" message in return such as "I can't do that because...", or "I don't want to do that because..." If he fails to complete the action or the message, he is "it" and carries on the game.

Variation: Have two or more "it's" simultaneously active.

"Who Stole My Swimming Suit" Or "A Little Play About 'I' Messages"

This play tells a story about "I" messages. It can be acted out with puppets or group members, but be sure to allow persons time to practice before they perform it for the group.

Characters:

Narrator
Sally   (a young girl)
Tim   (Sally's younger brother)
Mom   (Could also be played as dad, older brother, etc.)
Rex   (The family dog-optional)

Narrator: Sally and Tim love to go swimming. They like to swim outdoors, indoors, at the ocean, in the bathtub, or anywhere there is enough water to get wet. Today they are getting ready to go to the swimming pool, but there is a small problem. Let's listen in.

Sally: Hurry up, Tim. I'm all ready to go.

Tim: I *am* hurrying up, but someone stole my bathing suit and I can't find it!

Sally: What do you mean *stole* your bathing suit? You just forgot where you put it.

Tim: No, it's been stolen. I know it. I put it right on this hook and now it's gone.

Sally: Oh, you're so dumb. Nobody would want your old swimming suit anyhow.

Tim: You stop. I'm going to tell mom.

Sally: Tell her then and see if I care. (chanting) Timmy lost his swimming suit, Timmy lost his swimming suit.

Tim: That's it. I'm gonna tell on you and I hate you too.

Sally: You don't either. I'm your sister and it's bad to hate sisters.

Tim: You just wait and see. Maybe somebody'll steal *your* suit. MOM!!

Mom: Yes, what do you want?

Tim: My swimming suit has been stolen and Sally is talking bad to me, and I just *hate* her.

Mom: (calmly) OK, your suit isn't where it should be, you don't like the way Sally is talking to you, and you don't like her right now.

Tim: Right! I hate her!

Mom: Tim, I want you to tell Sally, not, me, what it is she is doing that you don't like. Please tell her exactly what you don't like and would you please start it out like this: "I don't like it when you..." and then finish it up with "because..."

Tim: But mom, she's talking mean to me.

Mom: Tell her, not me. And please tell her with a message that starts out with "I" and explains why you don't like it.

Tim: Well...I'll try. Sally, I hate it when you say I'm dumb and lost my suit because I didn't and I feel stupid when you say so.

Sally: Well, sometimes you *are* dumb.

Mom: Hey, wait a minute. How about *YOU* starting your message with "I" too, Sally?

Sally: Well, okay. I think you're... well... er... um...

Mom: I notice it's harder to say "I think you're dumb", then just to say "Your dumb". I wonder why that is?

Sally: Well, I really don't think he's dumb. He's my brother. It's just something to say, really.

Mom: Hey look, here comes Rex dragging something.

Tim: MY SWIMMING SUIT! Rex, give that to me.

Mom: Try an "I" message with Rex, would you Tim?

Tim: Hey, Rex old boy, *I Want My Swimming Suit!* Good boy! Hey there, you did steal it didn't you!

Sally: Do you mean "*I* see that you stole it?"

Mom: And Sally, do you mean "I see that I was wrong, and I apologize?"

Sally: Yeah, that's what *I* mean.

Tim: *I* want to go swimming.

Mom: *I* love your *I* messages, and *I'm* ready to go.

ARTS AND CRAFTS

"I" Texture Messages

Materials: Crayons
             Thin drawing paper
             Pencil
             Textured surface

Invite participants to make a simple outline drawing or design in pencil on the drawing paper. Then demonstrate how to hold the paper against a textured surface (e.g. a book cover, a flat rock, cement, etc.). Rub with the crayon only within the penciled area. The texture will transfer to the paper. Demonstrate using "I" messages such as: "I am now drawing my design; I am now rubbing with crayons; I now see the design in textured color, and I like it, or I am not satisfied and want to try again." Encourage participants to exchange ideas and to frame them in "I" messages, both positive and negative.

Dough Art

Use equal parts of flour and salt to make a dough mixture. Form it into "I" shapes and bake in the oven until golden brown. When cooled, paint the "I's" and use in a discussion, having each person hold up his "I" as he says his own, special "I" message.

Edible "I's"

Make a pretzel dough (see recipe in Appendix) and let members form pieces of the dough into "I's". Bake, and practice giving "I" messages while eating the edible "I's".

"I" Message Snacks

While preparing and eating a snack, try using only "I" messages. Discuss the use of "I" messages, and how they change conversation. Do you make it easier or harder to communicate while working on a common task?

Paper Airplanes

Make paper airplanes as a group. Let each person write "I" messages on the planes, be a pilot, and practice giving an "I" message with each throw of his paper airplane. Work together in encouraging each person to achieve his farthest flight, most loops, highest flight, etc. Encourage and reinforce all efforts to participate. Coach as needed.

✛ ✛ ✛ ✛

"I" Message Cartoons

Provide art materials. Let each person draw or cut out pictures to make cartoons. Write a script using "I" messages. Let each person share his cartoon with the group.

Allow time for each person to talk and for feedback from the group.

✛ ✛ ✛ ✛

"Rub-A-Dub"

Materials: Chalk, soft lead pencils or crayons
Paper
Cardboard for mounting

Assorted objects such as: zipper, rick rack, flat jewelry, small comb, various coins, paper clips, keys, leaves, paper doilies, nail file, emery boards, books with raised or indented cover designs, license plate, or any flat object with some raised parts. Letters may be drawn, cut out, and rubbed to make a word message.

Invite the participants to look for objects with surfaces which represent experiences or values to them (may be done just for fun without the values component). Place paper over the surface and rub with chalk, pencil, or crayon to secure transfer effect. Encourage the participants to look various places for objects to rub and to create their own set of rubbings. Encourage them to find "likes" as well as "dislikes" and to combine as they wish. Mount rubbings on cardboard. As leader, model with spontaneity and openness.

Share "I" messages around the circles or as appropriate. Encourage recognition and expression of values as well as shapes and textures.

✛ ✛ ✛ ✛

Sketching And Etching

Materials: Paper, paper plates or tag board
Crayons
Nail, unbent paper clip, or
    similar object for etching

Invite the participants to fill their paper surfaces with heavy crayon in design, multicolor, or plain. The entire surface is to be heavily crayoned. When this is complete, color heavily over the entire surface with *black* crayon. Now the creative part! Invite each participant to think of something to express in simple line drawing. Give scratch paper for planning if desired. Invite each person to draw a representation of something he actively likes or dislikes. Give each participant a nail or similar object with which to "etch" his drawing on the black surface. The black will come off, and the colors will show through whenever the surface is etched or scratched. Larger areas may also be scratched away for solid segments of the drawing. This is a simple, fun exercise to do. Provide extra materials for false starts, rips or tears.

Active listen any discouragement or frustration. Model the exercise. Pick up on the practice of "I" messages, either in the group or as individuals are creating. As leader, model "I" messages.

When all have completed their etchings, give each an opportunity to frame his "I" message about the etching to the group. Mount and display according to the wishes of the individual.

✛ ✛ ✛ ✛

"I" Boxes

Materials: One shoe box or the equivalent
              for each participant
              Glue
              Scissors
              Markers, crayons, etc.
              Variety of decorating material
              (glitter, yarn, colored
              construction paper, buttons,
              foil, cotton balls, colored
              fabric, ribbon, etc.)
              Magazines for pictures

1. Invite each participant to select a box and decorate it according to his own ideas and preferences. Provide ample materials for decoration. Each box is to have a flap or a slit into which messages written on paper can be inserted. Show the participants a "model" box so they will have some ideas about what they can do.

2. When all have had time to complete their decorating, invite each participant to write a positive "I" message to each other participant and deliver it through the slip or flat in the receiver's "I" box. Suggest that the message be written as a short letter such as:

> Dear Rick:
>
> I like it when you say "Hi" to me at school.
>
> > Sincerely,
> > Bob

Most groups will need some modeling from the leader in order to get into this in a productive way. One effective modeling technique is for the leader to write to each group member while they are doing their dec-

orating and then read his messages aloud after explaining part #2.

When all have received their messages, the exercise may proceed in at least two possible ways according to time and interest:

1. Give time for everyone to read his messages and to respond to the senders within the group. Then discuss as a group to consolidate the positive gains in self esteem and group rapport.

2. Invite each participant to take his box home and open one message each day. A visit or phone call to the sender from the receiver could be suggested as appropriate.

Encourage all positive interaction and active listen any negative feedback. Give one-to-one assistance to any one who is having problems with creating positive messages.

✛ ✛ ✛ ✛

"I" Patches

Materials: Patch material from old jeans,
              iron-on patches, band aids,
              pieces of fabric or whatever
              you can find
              Large needle
              Yarn or fabric markers

Invite participants to create their own positive "I" message about themselves. Each participant then can create a design or symbol to represent his "I" message. Encourage partic001pants to select the materials needed to create the design. Designs can be cut, stitchery executed, iron-on patches cut up to form designs to iron onto other iron-on patches which then can be ironed onto any- 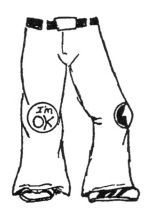 thing that needs a patch or a decoration (such as notebooks, clothing, wallets, etc.). A patch can even be framed to make a wall-hanging of significance. Share the "I" messages represented by the patch making.

✛ ✛ ✛ ✛

"I" Messages From Nature

Materials: Any forms of plant life which are flat (grasses, leaves, bark, weeds, etc.)
Waxed paper
Iron and plug-in

Invite the participant to cut two sheets of the waxed paper and to place their desired forms of plant life on the bottom sheet in whatever design they like. Cover with the second sheet of waxed paper so that the plants are sandwiched between the layers of waxed paper. Place a single thickness of newspaper over all layers, then iron with a warm iron, being sure to cover the entire area several times. The heat will seal the waxed papers together and will preserve the plant life. During the process, encourage each participant to self-rehearse with "I" messages such as: Now I am cutting the sheets of waxed paper; now I am arranging my plants; I like this arrangement; I do not like that arrangement; etc. Encourage participants to give "I" messages to one another as well as to themselves.

Variation: substitute small chips of various colored crayons for the plant life. A colorful picture will result.

CAUTION: Protect your work surface from wax and heat.

INDIVIDUAL CENTERS

"I" Message Center

Title a learning center "The 'I' Message Center". Let a person cut out magazine pictures and paste them on paper to illustrate the sentence:

"I feel _____ when you _____."

Allow the person to explain what he has created by asking him who "you" is and by guessing his feeling and the behavior.

Variation:

"When you _____ I feel _____."

"I like it when you _____."

"I don't like it when you _____."

"I am _____ because _____."

Active listen to his feelings, coach and reinforce.

"I" Wheels

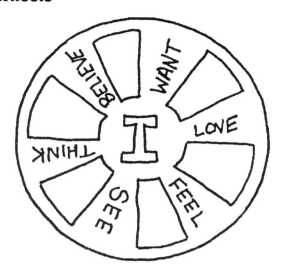

To set up an "I" Wheel learning center, make a cardboard circle and draw a large "I" on it. Now cut out strips of heavy paper and write words on them which "I" can do such as see, think, believe, want, understand, choose, love, feel, hear, hope, like, or dislike. Tape the words around the large "I"-like spokes on a wheel. A person can then choose a spoke and complete the sentence. For example, "*I like* peaches", or "*I hope* I will make the baseball team". Allow the person to discuss his "I" statements if he desires. Rotate the strips of paper to make other "I" messages possible. This activity may be done individually, in dyads, or in small groups.

BOOKS

Picture Books

Barrett, John M., **No Time For Me**.
Hazen, Barbara Shook, **If It Weren't For Benjamin**.
Sandberg, Inger and Lasse, **Come On Out, Daddy!**
Zolotow, Charlotte Shapiro, **The Quarreling Book**.

Fiction Books

Greene, Constance Clarke, **Your Old Pal, AL**.
Hogan, Paula, **Sometimes I Get So Mad**.
Park, Barbara, **Don't Make Me Smile**.
Perl, Lila, **Me And Fat Glenda**.
Snyder, Zilpha Keatley, **Come On, Patsy**.

Footnotes

[1]John O. Stevens, Awareness (Lafayette, California: Real People Press, 1971), p. 100.
[2]*Ibid.*, p. 74.

CHAPTER 6

Body Language

INTRODUCTION OF CONCEPT

We are always communicating; our bodies, facial expressions, and tone of voice often carry more meaning than the words we say. Therefore, conscious use of nonverbal communication is a very important part of effective communication.

Eye Contact

Eye contact is a powerful signal in body communications. Direct eye contact tells the receiver "I am with you; you are important to me". Little or no eye contact may communicate disinterest and rejection. It may also communicate a low self-concept to the other person.

Leveling

Physical "leveling" so that my eyes are not significantly above or below the other person's eye level is another important part of body language. Purposefully seeing a comparable "level" implies equality and tells the other person "we are equal in value and I respect your worth". Positioning yourself higher than the other person may be interpreted as placing that person at a disadvantage while the higher person takes power and a superior position. This may invite resentment.

Smiling

Smiling is also a cue which usually is interpreted by the receiver as acceptance, interest, and enjoyment. There is considerable evidence that direct communication accompanied by a smile is received more favorably and that the smile also has positive valence in attitude for the message sender. It enhances the communication and helps the sender feel happier about the message sent.

Open Body Language

Open body language (arms unclasped, legs not crossed) projects acceptance. Open palms tends to signal trust. Leaning slightly forward toward another person represents strong interest. These and other body cues can add enormously to the impact that a message carries.

Congruency

Congruency is matching our facial expressions, tone of voice, and body language with the verbal messages we give. It is possible to send conflicting body signals such as clenched fists and hard edge sound to the voice, with an incongruent smile on the face. This mixture of body and verbal cues confuses the receiver just as a mixture of positive and negative verbal cues is difficult to understand. Giving the same message with both words and body language projects a clear and credible communication. If all communication components are congruent, the impact of our message is strengthened, and honest communication is enhanced. An awareness and application of these cues will increase effective communication.

INTRODUCTION TO PARTICIPANTS

When we say words to another person, those words are only one part of the message we send. My words may say "It's okay", but my body, the look on my face, or my tone of voice may say something different. Can you think of some ways we "talk" with our bodies?

(DISCUSS)

Congruency

We usually speak words which have one meaning; however, unless our words and our body language of looks and movements say the same thing, the persons we talk to may get mixed up about what we really mean. For instance, if I say,

"I would like to eat lunch with you",

but then at the same time I frown, or I am looking down at the floor or out the window, you may wonder if I really mean what I said. It is as if I invite you to my house, but have the curtains pulled and the doors locked when you come, and I do not answer the doorbell or your knock. It is like saying you are not angry, but your face is tense, you are holding your breath, and your fists are doubled up. The way you look and act are not saying the same thing as what you are saying.

Eye Contact

Because what we do and how we look often tells people more than what we say, we are going to think about "body language" and how it works. Where we look with our eyes tells people a lot about what is going on with us. When we talk to someone but do not look at them, the message they get is that we don't want to be with them. When we turn away from them, they think we would rather talk to someone else or be some other place. If we frown, they may think we are angry at them or do not like them, even though we were not thinking that at all.

Smiling, Leveling, Open Body Language

If we smile, look at them, turn toward them, and lean toward them a little, unclasping our arms and uncrossing our legs, they are likely to think we like them and are interested in them.

Some people go around thinking that others are smarter and better than they are. This means that they may be a little scared of other people. Others put up a front to cover their uneasy feelings and act as if they "know it all" or "are better than others". These are usually the people who are the most scared of all.

A lot of people pull back from each other because they do not know how the other person will react to them, and they do not want to be rejected or turned down. It is as if down deep we all may want to be open, and visit each other's houses, but when we see signs that the curtains are closed or the door is shut, we do not know whether we are welcome. Body language which is open is like having the curtains and the doors of a house open with someone there to welcome you.

Would you like to find out about body language and how to let our bodies help us say what we really feel? Let us think of some messages we can send with both our bodies and words.

INTERACTION ACTIVITIES

Personality Exchange

Invite participants to pair up and exchange personalities for a short time. Encourage them to model the body language patterns, assume characteristics and try to "be" their partner without using words. After a short time, discuss the experience of "being" someone else. Then discuss how it felt to see someone "being" me. Invite participants to share insights and to discuss the experience with partners and in the larger group.

Incongruent Messages

To become more aware of congruency in communication, have persons in the group pair up and sit down facing each other. Ask them to deliberately cancel everything they say with a non-verbal message. Have them use gestures, facial expressions, tone of voice, laughter, and other non-verbal behavior to cancel their own verbal messages. Give them a few minutes to take turns doing this with their partners.

Ask them to sit quietly for a while and think about the experience. Discuss what methods they used to cancel messages. Do they recognize any of these methods as old patterns? Ask how it felt to cancel messages and to receive canceled messages.

Variation: Ask the partners to communicate using body language which emphasizes their meanings and is congruent. Discuss the experience. This exercise can bring awareness of the relationship between verbal and non-verbal communication.[1]

Find The Leader

Invite one participant to volunteer to leave the room so that she does not hear or see what is happening. While she is outside, have the group pick a temporary leader. When the player has been called back, have the group begin to clap. The temporary leader will then change from clapping to some other action such as whistling, twiddling thumbs, scratching an ear, or jumping on one foot. The leader may change actions at any time, but when the "it" player discovers who the leader is, then the leader is next to leave the room and the process is repeated. The exercise will serve to sharpen participants' perceptions of others' actions and of their own actions. Talk about the group experience in a circle and give everyone opportunity to speak.

The "Hug" Game

Whoever is "it" chases the other, attempting to tag one who would then be "it". However, a player is safe it she is hugging another player. After the group has played for awhile, require that three people must hug in order to be safe. Next try four, then five, until the whole group is hugging and the game dissolves. The game builds group dynamics, a sense of oneness, and can help the participants become more aware of their physical actions. Take time to sit down together in a circle and discuss the learning gained from the game.

We Can Do It... Together

Invite the participants to divide into pairs and give each pair one marker and one piece of paper. Without any exchange of words, they are to draw a picture together with the marker on the paper. Any non-verbal communication is okay. When the teams have finished, form a circle, display the pictures, and discuss the various processes used to create them. How are the decisions made? What part did body language play? How did the no-talking guideline affect the activity? How do the participants feel toward their partners? Discuss in dyads as well as in the group. Encourage insight and openness.

Stone, Paper, Scissor

Demonstrate to the group three symbolic hand signals:

1. Stone—a closed fist

2. Paper—hand open, palm down

3. Scissor—two fingers up, others down

Invite the participants to divide themselves into dyads (pairs). While facing each other, they are to count "one, two", pounding the right fist into the left hand on each count. On the count of "three", each makes one of the symbols with her right hand (stone, paper, or scissor). Stone crushes scissor, paper covers stone, scissor

cuts paper. Whoever made the more powerful symbol has gained one point. The game then proceeds as before in a rhythmic pattern. Keep track of points for fun and then discuss body language cues.

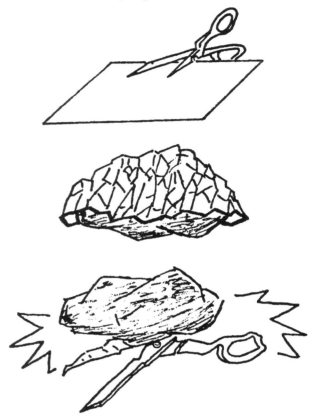

Variation: Divide participants into two teams. Map out "free" zones and explain signals. Before playing a unit, each team must huddle to decide which signal to throw on the count of "three". The teams then face each other in two long lines and throw their signals on the count of three. The team throwing the more powerful signal chases the other team, trying to tag as many persons as possible before they have reached the designated free zone. Those who were tagged are to join the other team. Continue playing until everyone is on one team. Sit in a circle to share learning gained from the game. Zero in on body language, feelings, and the use of "I" messages for communication.

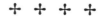

Frown-Off

Divide the participants into two teams who then stand facing one another in lines approximately three feet apart. Two players, one at each end of the line on opposite sides, begin the process as challengers. They each step out and walk toward each other, keeping eye contact until they meet in the middle. They are to proceed walking between the lines until they get to the end. The object is to make the walk between the lines without smiling. Meanwhile, players on the two teams are to do anything within their power, barring physical persuasion, to make the challengers laugh.

If the challenger makes it to the end of the line without cracking a smile, she may rejoin her team; however, if her facial expression shows the slightest amusement, she must join the opposite team at the end of their line. When everyone is on one team or when all players have run the gauntlet, the game ends.

This activity will help the participants to be aware of their power of choice and also of the power of influence toward a particular body language message (to laugh or not to laugh).

I Can't Talk... I Can't See

Divide the participants into groups of approximately six (make sure numbers are even in each group). Blindfold half of each group and instruct them to be "blind". Instruct the other half to be mute; they are not to speak.

Give each mute player a string and instruct her to communicate without words to the blind player that she is to tie the string around the waist of the mute player. The mute player is not to physically help complete the process. When all have completed this assignment, remove blindfolds and open a discussion time where each has opportunity to speak. Talk about the experience, guiding the group toward increased realization of the potentials of non-verbal communication. The activity promotes creativity in body language to achieve necessary communication.

Group Frown

Invite the participants to form a circle and to frown intensely. One player, appointed to be "it" moves around the inside of the circle trying to get a player to smile. "It" may say anything she likes to make any movements, but must not touch the other players. When one of the players breaks her frown and smiles, she becomes "it" and the previous "it" takes her place in the circle.

After a few minutes of this game, invite and encourage the participants to share their reactions and feelings. Was it difficult for them to continue frowning? How did they react to the person who was "it"?

Body Linguistics: Communication Styles

1. Invite the participants to form concentric circles with the same number of participants in each circle. Have each participant place her chair back to back with her partner's chair (inner and outer circle). Ask partners to move their chairs outward enough to place two to three feet between them.

    Give a topic for discussion (e.g. what I was doing just before I came to this meeting or how I would spend an extra $100). After about two minutes, direct partners to sit side by side to continue the discussion. After about two minutes, have them sit face to face.

    Discuss their experiences concerning communication barriers in each position. Brainstorm for situations where persons expect to communicate from the handicapped positions (e.g. side by side in the car; one at the sink, one at the table; back to back; etc.).

2. Ask the pairs to continue sitting face to face, but to assume the following three body postures while continuing their discussion:

    (1) Slouched in chair, arms and legs crossed and folded.

    (2) Sitting bolt upright, stiff and unbending.

    (3) Leaning forward, arms and legs unlocked, hands open slightly.

    Discuss their reactions to each of these three postures. Which was helpful to communication? Which was handicapping?

3. Sitting face to face and assuming an open posture

leaning slightly toward one another, ask them to designate which of them is A and which is B.

(1) Ask A to attempt to look B in the eye while B lets her eyes wander down or around the room while continuing the discussion.

(2) Ask B to attempt to look A in the eye while A lets her eyes wander down or around the room while continuing the discussion.

(3) Ask A and B to give each other direct eye contact while continuing their discussion.

Regroup the participants in a total circle to discuss the various reactions to body position (#1), body posture (#2), and eye contact (#3) as they relate to communication. Give time for all to express insights and experiences relating to the theme. Move the discussion toward group consensus as to the most facilitative position, posture, and eye contact for effective communication.

Variation: Use role plays to demonstrate and ask the role players to communicate their experiences and the group to comment.

✛ ✛ ✛ ✛

Body Talk

Invite participants to form a discussion circle with space enough between them to move freely. Introduce the idea of non-verbal communication or body language by asking them to respond non-verbally to the following statements:

1. You have just learned that your most prized possession has been stolen, but was found smashed and destroyed near your home.

2. You have just learned that $25,000 has been awarded to you.

3. You have just dropped a tray full of food in a crowded cafeteria.

4. You have been listening to a very boring, monotonous speaker for nearly an hour.

5. Someone you've wanted to get to know has just called to invite you to attend a party with her.

6. You are in a hurry to shop for one last ingredient needed to finish a recipe you are making for guests soon to arrive. Someone barges ahead of you and snatches the last package off the shelf, leaving you

without time or access to a replacement.

Vary for age level while providing a spectrum of emotional experience to model.

Discuss the variety of body reactions, their similarities and differences among the group members. Note that three major coping patterns tend to emerge: fight, flight, or give in. Model for participants by demonstrating your own body language reactions to the six situations; encourage openness, questioning, and insight.

Use the following questions to stimulate further discussion or role play:

1. Which emotions are easiest to allow others to see?

2. Which emotions are you most likely to want to hide?

3. What happens when we attempt to hide strong emotions from others?

4. What happens when we let out all our emotions to others?

Guide the discussion toward recognition that our bodies are always communicating to the people around us, that attempting to hide emotion conveys a "mixed message" but that total "dumping" is hardly appropriate either. Brainstorm a variety of ways to deal with strong emotion.

✛ ✛ ✛ ✛

The Ballooney Game

Write feeling words on small pieces of paper which can be inserted into deflated balloons. Insert them, matching the feeling to the color where possible. Blow up the balloons and tie them shut with the papers inside.

Invite the participants to sit in a circle around the balloons. One at a time, invite each participant to choose a balloon, pop it, and silently read the feeling written on the paper inside.

The participant then acts out her feeling non-verbally until someone in the group identifies it correctly and describes the body language which cued her to the feeling. Go around the circle till all have participated (if one person tends to dominate the responses, use a control mode which is non-rejecting such as pinning a star on her and stating that all starred persons are to wait until everyone else has had opportunity to respond).

The game builds consciousness of body language responses and provides feedback as to what conveys feeling more or less appropriately.

Shadow Strategy

    Materials: Lamp
                  Sheet

Darken the room after hanging a sheet in the doorway or elsewhere. Place an unshaded lamp 5-10 feet back from the hanging sheet. Between lamp and sheet, have persons in the group act out different emotions. The closer to the sheet the actor stands, the larger the shadow will be, and as she moves back, the shadow diminishes. Discuss non-verbal communication. Ask the participants what the various shadow pictures tell or show them. This activity dramatizes body language and presents another situation in which to learn about body communication.

Doormats, Dudes, And Doers

The purpose of the exercise is to secure awareness and practice in assertive behavior and to stimulate recognition of aggressive and unhealthy submissive behaviors.

1. Invite the participants to think of the most "doormat" person or personage they have ever know (if necessary, demonstrate from literature or media, e.g. "Eeyore" in *Winnie the Pooh*, etc.). Ask them to visualize the behavioral characteristics of that person, then have them move silently around the room, acting out those characteristics and being first-class doormats (if necessary, model as leader your perceptions of the doormat type). After a short period, ask all participants to "freeze" in their respective postures and to note the similarities of their positioning. Convene the group to list the behaviors and characteristics of doormatting. List also the mental attitudes associated with these behaviors (e.g. "Pardon me for living" etc.).

2. Invite the participants to think of the most aggressive person they have known and silently repeat the entire procedure. Explain that the aggressive person is threatening, judgmental, overbearing, combative, and defensive (note that any physical contact is not permitted). After the "freeze", again convene and list both behaviors and mental attitudes generated.

3. Describe the characteristics and behaviors of the assertive person with particular attention to the non-verbals such as eye contact, firm but comfortable body stance, and balanced, confident posture. Explain that the assertive person stands up for herself, but does not violate others to do so. Invite participants to think of a person who seems to fit the description of the assertive individual and to act out that style of behavior non-verbally. Have them freeze as before, observe and compare one another's behaviors. Convene and list behaviors and mental attitudes generated. Give time for discussion of the differences between the three behavior styles. Compare the lists derived from the exercise. If desired, role play behavioral styles in response to the following situations using verbal "I" messages and congruent non-verbals.

    (1) Someone has just elbowed his way into line in front of you. You have been waiting for an hour in the line and are about to be served.

    (2) Someone has borrowed your bicycle without asking permission and returned it to you with a flat tire.

    (3) A clerk has given you the wrong change in her favor, and there is a long line waiting behind you.

    (4) A teacher has given you a "D" grade and you believe that you have earned a "B".

Charades

To practice non-verbal communication, write messages on slips of paper, and ask group members to draw individually a message and act it out for the group to guess. Some examples are:

    What I want to be when I grow up

    My favorite TV show

    A song I've learned

A job someone in my family has

A kitchen utensil

A tool

Instruct them to use no words in the acting out, but to communicate the messages non-verbally.

Act It Out

Materials: Pictures of people and animals in many different poses such as standing, sitting, lying, kneeling, etc.

Show one picture to a person and ask her to do what the picture shows. Do not show the picture to the other players. Then, when the person is ready, let her act out the picture. Show five or six pictures to the rest of the group including the one being acted out and ask them to guess which picture is being portrayed.

What's That Expression

Have each person pick an expression or body posture which communicates a message. One by one, have them freeze into that position while the rest of the group identifies it. Discuss non-verbal communication.

Body Language Skits

Divide the group into pairs, and assign each person a characterization. Now give each group the same set of lines, and instruct them to act out the scene with the characterizations they have been given. The lines can be very simple with one person being #1 and the other #2. For example:

#1 Other person's name.

#2 Other person's name.

#1 Hi.

#2 Hello.

#1 How are you?

#2 I'm fine, how about you?

#1 I'm O.K., how are Steve and Ruth?

#2 They're well.

#1 How's the weather been?

#2 Why?

#1 Well, what did you want me to say?

Help each pair decide how to say the lines to convey their motives and situations. Use body language including tone of voice as well as the usual components of gesture, facial expression, stance, etc. The lines in each scene take on meaning because of the way the persons say them, not because of their content. This exercise will serve to demonstrate the power of body language to communicate messages regardless of the words spoken.

Possible Characterizations:

1. A convict just getting out of prison and meeting her son or daughter. She wants him/her to believe that she has changed, and the child wants her to know that everything will be O.K. Steve and Ruth are other children in the family.

2. A couple on a first date, set up blind by Steve and Ruth. The girl is embarrassed and not pleased with the situation, but the fellow is happy about the date.

3. A foreign exchange student just meeting her host/hostess for the first time. The student is very thrilled to be in the country, but the host/hostess is shy and somewhat fearful about having a stranger in her home. Steve and Ruth are the tour coordinators.

4. A family just moved into the neighborhood, and the teenager is going to meet the person her age who lives next door. She is anxious to make new friends, but the neighbor is defensive and cautious. Steve and Ruth are the neighbors who just moved out.

5. A girl and boy meeting accidentally at a party. They dated for a few months, then broke up and have not seen each other since. Both are uncomfortable and embarrassed with the situation. Steve and Ruth are a couple they used to double date with.

6. A person coming in for a job interview with a firm. She very much wants to get the job, but the secretary does not care to be helpful or pleasant. Steve and Ruth are other employees of the firm.

ARTS AND CRAFTS

Mr. Pipecleaner

Have each person create a stick figure with two or more pipe cleaners. They may use something for the head if they want to make their "person" a little more complex. Since Mr. Pipecleaner has two arms and two legs, he can be bent into many postures and form many body messages. Some ways to work with him might be:

1. Have a person cross Mr. Pipecleaner's legs as people often do and explain to them that this is "closed" body language. Now demonstrate "open" body language. Ask them to make Mr. Pipecleaner look sad, mad, or glad.

2. Ask persons to make their stick persons look happy, or in a hurry, or scared, or gloomy. Have them experiment and see which postures imply which emotions to them. You might also have them show Mr. Pipecleaner being bossy, or kind, or like someone they think is mean, or someone they think is nice.

3. Give each person a chance to explain what her stick person is being or doing and why. Active listen or paraphrase back what is said and perception-check to see if you understood what was meant. Make sure you understand before talking to the next person. Be supportive of each person's efforts.

Two-dimensional Body Language

Provide body length sheets of newsprint or butcher paper. Divide the group into pairs and ask one member of each pair to lie down on the paper in a position which suggests a message such as tiredness, energy, happiness, loneliness, or confidence. The other partner draws around the person and then the group plays a guessing game to figure out the message each body figure is portraying. Discuss body language emphasizing how body cues vary in different situations.

Happy-Face Shebang

Give each person a sheet of yellow stiff paper and some round objects with which to draw circles such as plastic cups, coins, or other round objects depending on what size you prefer.

Encourage her to outline and cut out a group of yellow circles which can be brought to life. Invite each person to draw in as many facial expressions as she has yellow circles. Ask her to label each one with the expression she was intending by either writing on the circles, or by attaching the circles to another sheet of paper of a different color which will serve as a frame. It is also fun to make a mobile out of the various faces. (These can be all of the same size, or could be varied in size for interest and/or emphasis. e.g. If I want to be happy most of the time, I make a happy face which is larger than my angry face!)

Yarn People

Give each person a sheet of stiff paper and an assortment of yarn pieces of varying colors and lengths. Provide a container of white glue for each group of three or four participants. Have them select a yarn color to represent a particular person, dip the yarn in the white glue, then arrange the yarn on the paper in the shape of a figure something like the gingerbread man outline. Invite the participants to place the head, arms, legs, feet, and other body parts in positions which give off particular messages such as:

I am in a hurry	I am hopeful
I am sad	I am discouraged
I am very tired	I am embarrassed
I am happy	I am angry
I am weak	I am bored
I am strong	I am excited

Allow the participants to use color and form to

demonstrate emotion or state of mind. Then give each person opportunity to "tell" what her figure or figures represent to her. This exercise is adaptable for persons who work quickly and may have time to do several figures while others may only complete one. When the yarn dries, the picture may be decorated further.

✝ ✝ ✝ ✝

Pretzel People

Make a pretzel dough (see recipe in Appendix). Allow time for dough to rise. Discuss body language and different meanings of body positions in terms of "open", "closed", etc. Shape the pretzel dough into different body positions to depict feelings and attitudes. Bake, eat and discuss.

✝ ✝ ✝ ✝

Make Up A New Identity

Provide pictures of happy and sad clowns, or mimes, some basic kinds of theatrical makeup such as lipstick, eyebrow pencil, rouge, and white face, and a large mirror. Let persons go to the makeup center individually or in pairs. Explain to them that our faces often show the world what kinds of persons we are. Ask them to think of a new way they would like to look to communicate a new message about themselves. They may then make up themselves or each other to illustrate the new role they have chosen. When they are done, ask them to show their new faces to the group and explain the new roles. Discuss with the group what our faces tell others about us. Give them the option of staying in the makeup for a while to have more time to feel the new face.

✝ ✝ ✝ ✝

Modeled Body Language

Post pictures demonstrating various forms of body language. Have modeling clay available and offer a person the opportunity to mold it into different body postures which she can interpret if desired.

Variation: Ask the person to make clay figures

which will complete this sentence: "This is me when I'm _____". (Others may guess what the completed word is.)

✝ ✝ ✝ ✝

Body Builders And Character Cut-ups

Divide the participants into pairs and explain that no words will be spoken or written during the first part of the game. Provide the following materials and any others which you think would be useful:

> various colors of paper
> glue
> staplers
> ribbons
> paper plates
> paper clips
> pieces of fabric (consumable)
> scissors
> plastics of various kinds
> paper punches
> aluminum foil
> scarves
> crayons
> newspaper
> scotch and masking tape
> needle and thread

1. Ask partners to designate themselves as A or B (using sign language), Instruct the "A's" to use any materials they wish to decorate their B partners in order to make them into a particular character. Then they are to demonstrate to their B partners who that character is, and how she or he is to act without words.

2. "B's" keep their decorations on, but now are to do the same for their A partners. Make sure that the supply of materials is ample and encourage them to really get into their characterizations. The "B's" are to instruct their A partners without speaking as to who the character is, and how she or he is to act.

3. A grand "character show" will then be held from a designated stage area and all participants are to guess who and what each character is depicting from this decoration and her body language. When all have performed and been identified, discuss the exercise including the frustrations of working without words. Allow the participants to keep their decorations if they wish.

BOOKS

Picture Books

Anderson, Hans Christian, **The Ugly Duckling.**
Ets, Marie H., **Talking Without Words.**
Keats, Ezra J., **Peter's Chair.**
Lionni, Leo, **Fish Is Fish.**
Lionni, Leo, **Swimmy.**

Fiction Books

Greene, Constance C., **The Ears Of Louis.**
Waber, Bernard, **You Look Ridiculous.**

Footnotes

[1]John O. Stevens, Awareness (Lafayette, California: Real
    People Press, 1971), p.115.

CHAPTER 7

Reflective (Active) Listening

INTRODUCTION OF CONCEPT

There is one sure response which can be offered to a person who is hurting, emotionally upset, or experiencing any kind of problem. This is called reflective or active listening. It is you following the other person's train of thought and when the person is unable to go further, you briefly reflect (state) back the *feelings* and/or *what has been said*. This makes it more possible for the other person to clarify feelings or thoughts, and then go further in expressing those feelings or ideas. The person can later come to a conclusion, make closure, problem solve or make decisions once there has been a change to express both feelings and ideas.

Silence, open body language, and nods of understanding, are all part of an accepting manner which will go far to convey to the sender that it safe to get feelings out as well as ideas. If the feelings are strong and anger or tears are expressed, the listener will feel the trust and know that previously unexpressed burdens are being expressed. This sense of trust is fundamental to building a lasting relationship with adults or youth.

It is important for the listener to avoid efforts to secure information or direct the conversation, but rather to accept the sender's feelings at full intensity and follow where they lead. When someone is upset or emotionally distraught, the process of expressing emotion and feeling is usually far greater in importance than the content of what is said. It is thus the listener's responsibility to listen to sender's feelings rather than only to the content of the message. A basic assumption of the listening skill is that each person can be his own best problem-solver (at least to begin with). Once a major share of the emotion has been expressed, solutions and decisions will be easier to find.

Some kinds of responses tend to block the sender and make it difficult to continue. We call these "roadblocks to communication."

Some roadblocks to be avoided during the listening process include:

1. Distracting, diverting, humoring.
    Example:
    > "You'll feel better tomorrow; let's go do something else."

2. Criticizing, name calling, ridiculing, joking.
    Example:
    > "You're crazy to feel bad about that."

3. Judging, moralizing, preaching.
    Example:
    > "You shouldn't feel that way."

4. Controlling, commanding, ordering.
    Example
    > "Stop talking about that."

5. Blaming, threatening, warning.
    Example:
    > "If you do that, you'll be sorry."

6. Analyzing, diagnosing, questioning.
    Example:
    > "It's obvious you are really messed up."

7. Consoling, ignoring problem, comforting.
    Example:
    > "Time will heal it all."

8. Giving advice.
    Example:
    > "Here's how to handle that."

For you to be an effective listener, three questions need to be answered affirmatively by you. These questions are:

1. Do I care about this person?

2. Do I have time, or am I willing to take time to listen now?

3. Am I able to shift attention away from myself (or my problems) and devote attention to this person?

If you can answer "yes" to these three questions, you will be in a good position to serve for that time and situation as an active and reflective listener. A good method for helping the sender proceed when progress is slow is to ask "Do you mean…" and fill in a short paraphrase of the feeling that have already been expressed. This is a "door opener" listening response because it helps the sender gather thoughts, but leaves the door open to continue.

Listening is an important skill to learn because it affirms the worth of another individual and carries the message that "I care", and "I believe in you". It becomes an essential building block in establishing mutual trust for enhancing any relationship.

INTRODUCTION TO PARTICIPANTS

What is a friend? What kinds of things do you like in your friends or like for them to do?

(TAKE TIME TO LET PARTICIPANTS LIST QUALITIES THEY LIKE IN THEIR FRIENDS.)

Part of being a good friend is *listening*, especially when something is bothering your friend.

When a person feels badly about something, it is helpful for that person to express it ("get it out") and talk about it *to a trusted* friend. It is as if my friend's house had its water pipes broken and a lot of water was backing up into the house. Bad things will happen in the house if the water does not get drained out. If I go over to help get the pipes drained out and get them working again, I've help a lot.

When we notice that a friend is feeling badly about something or if we listen while the friend expresses feelings, we are doing the very same thing as helping with the water pipes. One important part of listening, though, is letting the person work on the problem himself or herself, rather than just telling them what to do. The reason for this is that often that person knows what can be done to help more than we do. However, until the negative feelings (backed up water), are cleaned out, it will not even be possible to see or understand what can be done to improve the situation. So, we can help get a pump started to move out the water. If the pump gets stopped and there is still more

water (hurt, anger, pain, embarrassment, etc.), we can help the word pump a little by saying, "Do you mean…" and adding a short statement of what we just heard said or felt. Then, if we are quiet, the word pump (sharing of feelings and ideas) will usually start again. This is called a reflective or active listening, and it is an important part of being a friend.

Some things that we might do will block up our friend's pump and make it very hard to express feelings. We call these things "roadblocks". If we are listening to a friend, remember:

Do not criticize! Do not call names, or joke or ridicule either – – – – – – – **JUST LISTEN!**

Do not judge! Do not preach at or tell your friend what should or should not be done – – – – – – – – **JUST LISTEN!**

Do not blame! It does not matter who is at fault. Blaming will stop the talk – – **JUST LISTEN!**

Do not console! Sympathy will stop up the pump and even if your friend feels better for a little while, that old water will do harm – – – – – – – – **JUST LISTEN!**

Do not question for your own information! This will distract from where your friend needs to be concentrating – – – – – – – **JUST LISTEN!**

Do not tell them what they should do! That stops the flow of talk from the friend, and just makes you look like you know it all. You can't know it all for another person. They must learn for themselves – – – – – – – – – **JUST LISTEN!**

Do not try to divert or humor! That would be like inviting your friend to go downtown for a coke when the house pipes are dumping water all over the floor – – – – – – **JUST LISTEN!**

Do not order or command! If the friend can get the water cleaned out, seeing what can be done about it is possible. Until then, orders and commands add to the problem – – **JUST LISTEN**

Do not give advice or lecture! That would be like reading directions to repair plumbing when the house is already two feet under water – – – – – – – **JUST LISTEN!**

Do not analyze or diagnose! This will only give the impression that you want your friend to know how smart you are and how much you know

about the situation. Let the
feelings be expressed   – – –   **JUST LISTEN!**

By now, you may have gotten the idea the best thing you can do for your friend who has broken plumbing (fear, hurt, anger, resentment, embarrassment, etc.) is to be there and to *listen*. The exit pump of words will work okay if you help prime the pump just a little from time to time. If you help by repeating some of what has been said, your friend's feelings will continue to be expressed as long as is needed for that day. After that, your friend may want help in solving the situation, but ONLY after the friend has expressed most of the feelings and ideas.

A good friend does what is best for another friend when that person is troubled. This means letting the friend do most all of the talking.

We can learn how to listen without blocking, and the following activities will give you some practice in how to do it.

INTERACTION ACTIVITIES

Listening Lab

Invite each participant to complete three of the following four sentences or similar statements:

1. I have the best feelings about myself when…

2. I have the worst feelings about myself when…

3. I like to be in a group of people when…

4. I don't like to be in a group of people when…

Present or review active or reflective listening including roadblocks to avoid, attending behavior, door-openers, listening for feelings, etc. Then divide into threesomes (tryads). Ask group members to designate themselves as A, B, and C.

Instruct A to B to focus on C and be his listeners for three minutes as C shares his feelings and responses to the questions. A and B are to give their full attention to C through body language, door-openers and silence. Then A or B is to reflect, using one of the "starter" phrases such as "Do you mean…", "Is it that…", or "It sounds as if you…"

The leader is to indicate by signal the end of the three minutes and at that time instruct C and A to focus

on B in the same manner. At the end of three minutes, the leader will indicate by signal, and B and C will then focus on A as indicated above.

At the end of the listening period, ask for feedback on the experience of being the listener and of being the sender. Encourage negative as well as positive feedback; some will see the exercise as awkward, fake, or phony. Active listen their discomfort and remind them that every new skill seems awkward at first.

Variation: Same exercise but use only dyads; A and B.

Now I Hear You... Now I Don't

1. Invite the participant to divide themselves into dyads with each dyad designating one of its members as A and the other as B. Instruct all the A's to think of a topic which is important to them and be ready to tell B about it. Instruct the B's to be silent, unresponsive, avert their eyes, and slowly move away. Give about two minutes for A and B to interact in this manner. Then reverse the roles with B's talking and A's being non-listeners.

Sit in a circle and discuss the activity, giving time for all to share their feelings about not being listened to and about being a non-listener. Give full opportunity for the feelings of rejection, resentment, anger, disappointment, or embarrassment to be expressed.

2. Now, repeat the sequence, but this time ask the partners to be attentive listeners to one another, giving eye contact, open body posture, smiles, and nods of acceptance. Give the same full amount of time as was given in sequence #1. Coach any who seem unaware of what is expected.

Reform the circle and discuss the second part of the activity and the differences between the two experiences. This activity is a powerful experience in recognizing the contrast between listening and non-listening effects upon the sender.

Listening Circles

Invite the participants to form an inner and an outer circle with the same number of persons in each. Have the circles face each other and widen the circle enough that conversation is possible without interference. Explain that a topic will be given for each pair to discuss with the inside person speaking first and the outside person being the active listener and then reversing the process. Review the principles of active listening given in the introduction and answer any questions before beginning.

In order to remind the pairs who is the sender at a given time, ask them to use a pencil or some familiar object as a "conversation piece". The person holding the "conversation piece" can talk, and is the sender; the other person is the listener. Give three minutes for A to hold the conversation piece and be the sender with B the receiver. Then call time and allow three minutes for B to hold the "conversation piece" and be the sender while A is the receiver-listener.

At the end of the each six minute sending-receiving period, rotate the outside group one or two persons and give a new topic of talking.

Suggested topics:

1. Tell about a favorite sport or game.

2. Share about someone important in your life when you where younger.

3. Tell of a time when you felt left out or rejected by a group or individual.

4. Describe the first home your remember and your feelings about it.

5. Tell about a time when someone misunderstood you and how you felt.

6. Tell about how you looked and felt at the age of 5-7.

7. Tell how you see yourself as different now and how you see yourself as the same.

When four or five topics have been discussed, discuss the experience as a group and encourage sharing. Ask each person to consider: Was it easier to talk or to listen? With which partner did I feel most comfortable? Which subjects were most and least comfortable for me to discuss? Encourage everyone to speak concerning the experience.

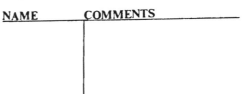

Active Listening Checklist

Active Listening
Checklist

Somebody's hurting and I want to help.
Do I care about this person?
Do I have time or will I take time to hear this person?
Am I able and willing to shift my own problems to the backround to devote my attention to this person?

If "yes" to all three, I am ready to listen!

NAME	COMMENTS

I must remember to tune into this person's feelings – to accept where he/she is coming from.

Active Listening Checklist

This poster (see end of chapter) lists the three questions a person must be able to answer positively before he can be an effective active listener. Discuss the checklist and have a practice active listening session by:

1. Dividing into dyads.

2. Asking one person to be "A" and the other to be "B".

3. Asking the "A's" to think of something in their lives which they would like to be different.

4. Inviting the "A's" to explain to the "B's" what they are thinking (allow about two minutes).

5. Instructing the "B's" to wait until "A" partner is silent, then to say "Do you mean..." and to rephrase what they have heard "A" say to "A's" satisfaction.

Reverse the process by exchanging roles and beginning again at #3 with "B's" sending and "A's" receiving.

Listening Practice

Prepare for a discussion of values by setting up opinion thermometers on two sides of the room. Label one "strongly agree" and the other "strongly disagree". Now present a series of topics to which everyone will react by placing themselves somewhere on the opinion thermometer. For example: "Persons should be allowed to drop out of school at whatever age they desire". Ask individuals to position themselves in the room near the thermometer with which they identify. They will stand close or further away depending on the intensity of their feelings. When all are positioned, have a person at one end state his feelings and beliefs about the question in "I" messages. The next person must restate the first person's ideas before stating his own. Continue until all have restated and expressed opinions.

Topics suggested are:

1. Children should have a say in the hiring and firing of teachers.

2. Chocolate ice cream is the best ice cream there is.

3. Ministers and social workers should be paid as much as pro baseball players.

4. Television commercials should be banned.

5. Everyone should be required to give a period of service to the country, either military or other.

(Use any other topics which will elicit strong feelings or reactions from the group.)

Roadblocks To Active Listening

Explain the basis of reflective or active listening and its purpose to the group (see the description at the first of the chapter). Prepare cube shaped blocks out of whatever you have handy (foam rubber, covered cereal boxes, cardboard cartons) and print a roadblock title on each one. Some possible roadblocks are:

distracting	moralizing	reasoning
criticizing	controlling	advising
name calling	blaming	probing
ridiculing	analyzing	praising
judging	consoling	
preaching	sympathizing	

Line these roadblocks up into an obstacle course,

and then ask for a volunteer to try the course. Divide the rest of the group into two teams. Have one group be the roadblockers who will sit down on the right of the roadblocks, and the other be the active listeners, who will sit down on the left of the roadblocks. As the volunteer approaches the first roadblock, he states his problem, and the first roadblocker gives a response using the first roadblock as distracting ("Oh, let's go get a coke") or criticizing ("You're being dumb to let that bother you") etc. The volunteer must stay at that roadblock until someone from the left side can active listen him. Then he can move on to the next roadblock, and repeat the procedure. Change volunteers in the middle if necessary. Explain that active listening can begin with "Do you mean…". or "Is it like…?"

Active Listening Exercise

Divide the group into units of three to five members. Assign a topic for discussion about which group members will have thoughts and feelings. Tell them that there will be a special listening rule for the discussion that before a person can speak, he must first describe the previous speaker's thoughts and feelings to that person's satisfaction. When the previous speaker indicates that his ideas and feelings are accurately reflected, the next speaker can go on.

To illustrate the activity, give the speaker a small

object such as a paper cup or ball. This object signifies the right to speak. The speaker holds it until he has spoken and the next person has accurately reflected his thoughts, and then he passes the ball to the next speaker. As the person who just did the listening receives the object, he becomes the next speaker.

✛ ✛ ✛ ✛

Door Openers

Discuss door openers with the group. Explain that these are used to tell a person who is having a problem that the listener cares and is willing to listen. Brainstorm a list of door openers such as:

"Do you want to talk about it."

"Sounds like you've got something on your mind."

"I'd like to hear about it."

"Want to talk?"

Divide the group into two equal parts. Group one will remember a recent time when they felt a strong emotion such as joy, fear, anger, or embarrassment and will take turns walking up to a closed door and stating these feelings. Members of group two are on the other side of the door. As a member of group one states his feelings, a member of group two opens the door, gives his door opener statement, and moves with his new partner to a corner of the room to talk about the feelings. Model the process to show how the exercise works.

✛ ✛ ✛ ✛

A New Way To Experience It

List a group of common experiences, linking them with senses which are not their usual perceptual routes such as:

The look of warmth

The sound of the sun setting

The feel of birds singing

The look of a siren (police or ambulance)

The smell of rain on a hot pavement

The feel of light shining down a dark pathway

The sound of cold

The feel of thunder

The sound of falling snow

The feel of a dog's barking

The look of fingernails across a blackboard

The feel of a train thundering past

Invite participants to choose a "new way to experience" and to interpret it for the group by pantomime, music, art, words or any other medium which can project feelings. Encourage them to reinforce one another by making reflective or active listening statements such as "I see that you enjoy the sunrise", or "You seem uncomfortable with the fingernails on the blackboard", etc.

✛ ✛ ✛ ✛

Reflective Listening Skits

Discuss reflective or active listening and the roadblocks which hinder listening. Divide the group into pairs, and let each pair choose a roadblock (see descriptions at beginning of chapter). Give them time to plan and present a roadblocked situation and then to act out the same situation using reflective listening skills. Discuss how it feels to give and receive both roadblocks and reflective listening.

✛ ✛ ✛ ✛

Four Roles

People often tend to relate to each other in one of four ways:

1. Placater—gives in to anyone and thinks that every-

thing is his fault.

2. Blamer—everything is someone else's fault.

3. Irrelevant—distracts in every possible way.

4. Computer—see only facts and not feelings.

Explain these to the group and then divide them into teams of four persons. Ask them to decide who is person "A", "B", "C", and "D". Write down which of the four roles person "A", "B", "C", and "D" are to play in the first round, and instruct them to assume the characteristics of that role. Give the group a task to do while playing the roles. After round one, shift roles. Do four rounds so that everyone gets to try each role.

Discuss how each person felt in the roles and how they each see themselves responding in real life. Model reflective listening during the discussion by reflecting their feelings and ideas.

Possible tasks:

1. Decide how to spend the next half hour.

2. Plan a family picnic.

3. Discuss how the group could spend a $15.00 gift certificate. (The task is unimportant except as a vehicle for portraying these roles.)

Variation: Let each person on the team choose an age and family role such as mother, grandfather or brother. They may then relate as a family with each person using the role he was assigned for that round.[1]

✛ ✛ ✛ ✛

From Roadblocks And Typical Types To Reflective (Active) Listening

Present the purposes and process of Reflective or Active Listening to the participants, giving strong emphasis to the meaning of "roadblocks". Post a list of the "roadblocks" and "typical types" where all can see them.

Roadblock	*Typical Type*
Advise	Lawyer
Command	General
Moralize	Reformer
Analyze	Psychiatrist
Criticize–Judge	Judge
Warn–Threaten	Police Officer
Divert–Flowery Praise	Florist
Probe–Question	Reporter
Quote Past Experience	Historian
Console–Sympathize	Mortician

Supply pencil and paper for each participant and ask them to number three columns from 1-10. At the top of the first column, ask them to write "roadblocks", at the top of the second column "typical type", at the top of the third "R-L/A-L" (Reflective and Active Listening). Read the following script, giving time for the participants to write in the roadblock and the typical type. When this is completed, go back through the statements, get their ideas, and discuss. There may be more than one "right" answer; the point of the exercise is to give them a way to become aware of roadblocking responses.

Go through the exercise again as a group; coach and encourage as you ask for Reflective-Active Listening responses. Give time for note-taking and discussion.

Variation: Give the group time to write in a reflective-active listening response to each first statement. Call for them as statements are reread; coach and discuss.

Script:

1. I'm worried. That's a hard test we're having tomorrow. Oh, forget it. Let's watch some TV and get something to eat.

_____	_____
Roadblock	Typical Type

2. I'm so mad I could punch my little brother's lights out! He put a crack in my new guitar.

   Well, it's no wonder the way you leave it laying around all the time; keep it in its case on a high shelf and stuff like that won't happen.

_____	_____
Roadblock	Typical Type

3. I'd like to talk to her (him) but I'm scared I'll say something dumb.

   Listen! Just do what I tell you, and you'll have it made.

_____	_____
Roadblock	Typical Type

4. I don't understand this assignment. It's a bunch of garbled junk to me.

You never take notes. You ought to keep a notebook for your assignments and write everything down right when the teacher say it like I do.

_____   _____
Roadblock   Typical Type

5. I'm just out of it today.

You're an introvert type; it probably runs in your family.

_____   _____
Roadblock   Typical Type

6. This is such a dumb school. I'd like to walk out of here and never come back.

I know just how you feel. Last year I felt just like that. It was awful. I nearly went bananas, believe me!

_____   _____
Roadblock   Typical Type

7. I'm afraid I didn't make that last cut on the ball team. Boy, I really wonder how it's gonna turn out.

Who was there that day? What time was it when you got through? Was the coach wearing his blue blazer or the black one?

_____   _____
Roadblock   Typical Type

8. I'd like to try out for a part in the play, but I don't know if I'd make it. I feel kinda scared.

If you don't get your hair fixed different, you sure won't make it. I can tell you one thing, that mop top you're wearing would wreck you for any decent part.

_____   _____
Roadblock   Typical Type

9. My mom's pretty sick; I'm scared something's really wrong with her.

Oh, don't worry. I know how you feel. It'll be okay. Just calm down. Here's some Kleenex.

_____   _____
Roadblock   Typical Type

10. I want to learn to skate; I think it would be fun, but I feel embarrassed getting out there and maybe falling down and everything.

Don't try it. You don't have the right build for it. You'll just make a sap of yourself anyhow.

_____   _____
Roadblock   Typical Type

Check with the following answers. Some blanks may have more than one possible Typical Type with its accompanying roadblocks:

1. Florist
2. General
3. Attorney
4. Reformer
5. Psychiatrist
6. Historian
7. Reporter
8. Police Officer
9. Mortician
10. Judge

✦ ✦ ✦ ✦

Listen On The Phone

Provide phones that ring and have a dial tone or a busy signal. Persons can actually hear one another through the receiver (there is often no charge for borrowing this equipment from local telephone companies). Use them to practice and sharpen listening skills with each other. Have the group prepare posters which will remind the user of active listening skills and post them around the phones. Make the posters positive such as: "Do you mean...", "Active listen to a friend", or "Give a door opener". If real phone equipment cannot be secured, toy phones may be used.

ARTS AND CRAFTS

Active Listening Ears

Invite each participant to design two ears about three times as large as life size and cut them out of construction paper. Also have each person cut out a band about one inch wide and long enough to fit around his head. Staple the ears to the band, let him decorate the ears as he desires and wear his "ears". Discuss his listening ears, and how they help him remember to hear. This activity is a reminder that listening is important.

+ + + +

Crackled Paper Crayon Resist

Materials: Crayons
              Manila paper
              Pencil
              Watercolors
              Brush

Make a light drawing in pencil on manila or heavy wrapping paper. Using the pencil lines as a guide, draw lines and shapes with the crayon, allowing areas of the paper to show through. Crumple the paper into the smallest possible ball. Smooth out the paper and paint its entire surface with watercolor paint. The paint will be absorbed by the uncolored paper and resisted by the wax crayon, creating a web-like pattern. Use the experience of creating a picture as a take-off point for a listening exercise. Have persons discuss the pictures with a friend and reflect feelings stated by each other. Explain that a reflective listening response can begin with "Do you mean…".

+ + + +

Kooky Krayons

Materials: Crayons
              Tape
              Paper

Invite participants to choose from an array of crayons, picking out three colors which fit their mood for the present. Show them how to tape the crayons together and then to draw with them on the paper in an expression of their feelings at that moment, when they are happy, when they are frustrated, and any other situations you wish to include. Kooky pictures will appear. Encourage the participants to talk about their pictures and active listen to them as a demonstration of caring and good will. Encourage them to listen to one

another's feelings and perceptions without roadblocking. Encourage and reinforce all efforts.

+ + + +

B.I.C. (Because I Care) Jewelry

Materials: Construction paper, several
                  colors
              Pencil and scissors
              White glue
              Sandpaper
              Shellac or clear nail polish
              Brush
              Electric drill
              Leather thong, chain, or
                  piece of twine

Invite participants to sketch a shape they would like for their piece of jewelry (pendant in heart shape, listening ear, apple, arrow, raindrop, etc.)

Cut about thirty of these shapes from various colors of construction paper, using whatever colors are preferred. Glue the shapes on top of each other, making sure each is thoroughly stuck to the one underneath it. Allow the glue to dry for approximately 24 hours. Sand around the edges at an angle to bevel and give interesting shape. Sanding does not have to be even. Sand some on top and even down through several layers to reveal various colors. *The sanding will take considerable time;* allow enough time for it. The more sanding that is done, the more beautiful the end result.

Coat the jewelry with at least two layers of clear nail polish or shellac. Use an electric drill to make a small hole clear through and hang on a thong, chain or piece of twine. Beautiful!

During the gluing period, ask each participant to share "how I feel when I cut and paste this color". Generate active listening responses from the people near him. While sanding, encourage active listening concerning feelings (joy, frustration, etc.).

At completion time, invite everyone to express his feelings about the whole project and his plans for what he has made. Structure active listening as seems best for the group, making sure that everyone is heard and validated by a listening response. As leader, model the project, the open expression of feelings, and the listening. This is a project to be extended over three or more group meetings.

✛ ✛ ✛ ✛

Adding Machine

Materials: One or more rolls of adding
                   machine tape
                   Scissors, stapler
                   Felt tipped pens or pencils

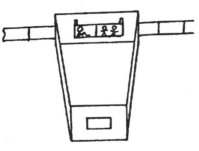

The shape of adding machine tape invites creative uses. Here are some to be adapted to active listening practice.

1. Invite participants to create in ones or twos a comic strip of an active listening event (e.g. angry person, friend responds with active listening).

2. Create a movie to "run" through a shoe-box projector with drawings to depict the active listening scene and participants voices to give sound effects.

3. Make a "mini-mural" depicting any kind of "feeling scene". Give creators the opportunity to tell their feelings concerning the scene and to be active listened by the group.

4. Use it to decorate or bind up a partner and then "listen off" his feelings.

✛ ✛ ✛ ✛

A "Listening" Collage

Materials: Large piece of cardboard
                   or wood
                   Glue
                   Pictures, magazine, photos, etc.
                   Materials for drawing
                   Fabric, string, yarn

Invite the participants to think about listening and how much they like to be heard as well as to hear. Ask them to collect "pieces" for their collages which relate to this idea. The emotions, experiences, and feelings which we want to tell about and hear about make good subject matter too. Cut-out letters, bits and pieces of music, poetry, songs, colored fabric, fur, or whatever is available will be fine.

Lay out the collage on the cardboard or wood, moving things around until the arrangement is pleasing to the creator. He may want to hunt up or create more parts; allow time as needed.

Glue the parts in place, making sure that corners are securely stuck down. When all is dry, coat with shellac if desired. Give each person time to tell about his collage and answer questions. Invite anyone to ask questions and to give a reflective response to the answer.

Some opener questions:

How do you feel about your collage?

What would you like to have different?

What do you like best about it?

Do you feel happy when you look at some parts?

Do you feel angry or sad when you look at some parts?

Variation: The collage form can be used in hundreds of ways for varying subject matter. The content is not the focus of this exercise; it is the feeling and the listening response to those feelings which are important. The investment of time and energy will evoke good emotional material for listening if opportunity is given.

✛ ✛ ✛ ✛

Painted Faces On Rocks

Materials: Smooth rocks
                   Acrylic paints
                   Brushes

Invite participants to find rocks in different sizes and shapes. Place newspapers in the work area and clean and dry the rocks. Encourage participants to paint with acrylic paints (use bright colors, quick drying, which can be cleaned with water). Encourage participants to paint faces showing different feelings. Use the rock collection to illustrate stories or role play feelings. Use the feelings generated and expressed for an active listening activity. Model, then invite the participants to respond in a cooperative listening mode.

✝ ✝ ✝ ✝

Pointers With Pointillism

Materials: Light colored construction paper
              Crayons
              Chalk

Pointillism is a way of making a color by combining tiny points of other colors. To color an area orange, you fill it with points or dots of yellow and red. In this technique, only points are used, no lines.

Prepare a design or a picture by sketching it lightly with chalk on construction paper. Color each area using pointillism or making "dots" of color. You can mix and match as you like and have fun creating new colors. The intensity of the dots will also vary the effect. When the picture is completed, erase the chalk. The picture will look different from a short distance away.

Practice active listening by telling about your experiences in creating your picture and letting others respond reflectively. Do the same for them.

✝ ✝ ✝ ✝

Basic Reflective Listening

Materials: Cards or strips of cardboard
              approximately 4" x 11"
              Markers or crayons

Explain to the group what some of the "lead-in" responses are for reflective listening (see  below). Do a role play or demonstration to illustrate how these work. Invite each participant to design his own set of "lead-in" cards to take home and post where he can see them to help him remember. Encourage creativity and individualism in the decorating process. The following are appropriate "lead-in":

"Do you mean…"

"Are you saying…"

"Could it be…"

"You're feeling…"

"Is it that…"

"Would you like to talk about it?"

The symbol of a listening ear may be helpful to remind the participant of the social uses of these phrases. Give time for group practice in using them.

INDIVIDUAL CENTERS

"Being My Own Active Listener"

Give a participant a tape recorder, instruct him in its use, then invite him to tell the recorder a feeling in one or two sentences. He may then replay the tape and give an active listening response to himself.

If a child is given privacy and the assurance that he can erase whatever he tapes, the tape recorder can serve effectively for him to vent feelings. The idea of active listening himself adds practice in the skill-building.

✝ ✝ ✝ ✝

Aluminum Foil Sculpturing And Listening

Materials: Aluminum foil
              Optional: tape, glue, straight
                         pins, paper clips, markers,
                         scraps of fabric, paper

Introduce the foil as a medium for expressing feelings. The participant may crumple his general supply of foil into a shape which represents his feelings in the present or a past time. He may then "active listen" the shape. When that emotion is expressed and listened, the foil may be reshaped as many times as desired. Allow the child as much privacy and as little supervision as possible for this exercise in order to give him opportunity to vent and process his feelings. The use of additional decorative or shaping materials is entirely optional.

Variation: Let several participants shape foil and then take turns talking and active listening for feelings expressed in the process and by the finished product.

✝ ✝ ✝ ✝

Do You Mean...? (An Exercise On Tape)

Prepare a cassette tape with a series of problem statements followed by thirty seconds of silence and then an explanation. The user can listen to the statement and formulate his response during the silence. The explanation will help him understand the effectiveness of his response.

Examples of problem statements to tape:

(Child's voice) "I feel terrible! I missed the bus this morning and my mother had to leave work to bring me to school. I just hate to have that happen."

(Thirty seconds of silence)

(Adult Voice) "If you understood that the speaker felt disappointed, upset, irritated and just plain terrible, you are right. Your response to him might have been, 'Do you mean that your day just started off wrong, and you still feel terrible?'."

Prepare as many similar situations as you like. These will provide individuals with practice in active listening. The use of an earplug will remove the sound distraction for others.

BOOKS

Picture Books

Berger, Terry, **A Friend Can Help.**
Guifoile, Elizabeth, **Nobody Listens To Andrew.**
Vigna, Judith, **Gregory's Stitches.**
Zolotow, Charlotte Shapiro, **The Hating Book.**

Fiction Books

Boutis, Victoria, **Katy Did It.**
Charnley, Nathaniel and Betty Jo, **Martha Ann And The Mother Store.**
Giff, Patricia Reilly, **Today Was A Terrible Day.**
Hobby, Janice Hale, **Staying Back.**
McLendon, Gloria Houston, **My Brother Joey Died.**

Footnotes

[1]Virginia Satir, Peoplemaking (Palo Alto, California: Science and Behavior Books, 1972), p. 63-71.

Active Listening Checklist

Somebody's hurting and I want to help.

Do I care about this person?

Do I have time or will I take time to hear this person?

Am I able and willing to shift my own problems to the backround to devote my attention to this person?

If "yes" to <u>all</u> three, I am ready to listen!

NAME	COMMENTS

I must remember to tune into this person's feelings – to accept where he/she is coming from.

CHAPTER 8

Problem Solving

INTRODUCTION OF CONCEPT

A good question to ask before attempting to find a solution to any interpersonal situation is, "Who owns the problem?" When someone is experiencing difficulty or is not getting needs met, we conclude that that person "owns" the problem. Sometimes two or more people are involved in a problem situation or a decision. When this is the case, everyone who is affected by the problem must be involved in deciding what to do about it. The process called "problem solving" will provide one way to search for solutions acceptable to everyone involved. This method has a high probability of cooperative follow-through by all concerned.

Here are six major steps in problem solving.

1. *DEFINE THE PROBLEM.* If time and care is taken for each participant to be heard and the problem is fully defined, the other four steps will proceed with much greater ease. Problem definition is extremely important. This is the chance for a creative statement and definition of the problem. Often, how a dilemma is stated sets the stage for how solvable it can be at a later stage of the problem solving process. It is important for each individual to state personal needs and for all to listen so that the full extent of each need is clarified. If there is more than one problem or decision, clarify which is of the most immediate importance and then proceed to solve the problems one at a time. When the problem is defined to everyone's satisfaction (using *reflective listening* and *"I" messages* when needed), move to the next step.

2. *BRAINSTORM FOR SOLUTIONS.* Encourage each participant to suggest many solutions; work for volume and scope. Have someone write down all ideas but *do not evaluate* at this point. This section is also very important. It is the chance to see parts of two or more ideas merge in the synthetic synergy of a cooperative search for good (great) answers to real problems. But remember, *DO NOT CRITICIZE* or evaluate any idea here no

matter how far out it may be. Strive for as many ideas as possible and even write down the ideas that seem impossible. It may be necessary for these to be expressed before other possibilities will be identified. Sometimes unusual ideas spark feasible solutions, so let the ideas roll. This is one way that high levels of creativity can be taught and fostered. When everyone has suggested every idea that can be thought of, move to the next step.

3. *EVALUATE THE SUGGESTED SOLUTIONS.* Look at each solution generated in the brainstorming step and give time for discussion and evaluation. Everyone who will be affected by the result is to have the power of veto. Keep all possible solutions which are seen as "ok" by all group members. If no acceptable solutions are found, go back to step one; however, remember to encourage creativity by accepting all ideas and combining solutions to come up with acceptable compromises.

4. *CHOOSE THE SOLUTION.* Select from among the best possible solutions the one or combination of ideas which seems most feasible and acceptable to all. Securing group consensus (agreement), for this is an important key to cooperation from all in the implementation of the solution. Anyone who is left feeling ignored and unwilling will be much less likely to be cooperative later with the process. Do not vote in problem solving; *everyone* must be either satisfied or okay with a compromise to be willing to cooperate. This most certainly includes children and youth!

5. *IMPLEMENT THE SOLUTION.* Decide who will do what, when, where, and how to implement the solution. Again, full agreement in consensus as to how it will be carried out is necessary for success. Be sure to get the investment of the people who will be doing the implementation and get established a time line for putting the solution into place.

6. *CHECK BACK.* Ask each person involved to make a commitment to the plan by setting up a time for

check back to see if the solution is working out adequately.

Problem solving may appear to be long and involved at the outset, but it is a relatively short method of finding solutions which will work for participants.

It is simple for people who hold power to impose power on the ones who do not. Sooner or later, however, the weaker ones will resent the repeated power play, and will be likely to sabotage implemented solutions imposed by power. When everyone is invested by having a part in the decision making and implementation, each is much more likely to be satisfied.

Problem solving can be a very important tool in fostering friendship between participants, peers, and adults. It thus becomes an exercise in relationship building. Each successful group process of looking for and finding solutions becomes a part of creative socialization for the participants. This is a invaluable process.

INTRODUCTION TO PARTICIPANTS

Sometimes we find that we have problems or decisions which are not just ours alone but which involve someone else, or even a group of people. It is as if some neighbors wanted to do something about a problem which included all of them.

For example, "What shall we do to get to know each other better"; or "How can we make our street safer so people will not get hurt?" If everyone who is interested will meet together, they can find some ways to make things better for all.

The first thing we can do is to get everyone who is involved to sit down together. We will need someone to take notes on paper and someone else to be in charge, so we will not all talk at once and will have our ideas written down for later discussion. Then we are ready to go about solving problems and making decisions.

1. Let each person express himself or herself about what is happening and what the problem is all about. We will only be able to work on one problem at a time, so decide which problem needs to be solved first. When we've heard from everyone and have stated the problem so that everyone agrees what it is, we can go on.

2. Our next step is to look for solutions. This is

sometimes called *brainstorming*. This means that everyone will be free to give ideas on what to do about the problem, no matter how unusual their ideas may be. The secretary will write them all down, and we will not stop until everyone has had a chance a give every single idea that can be suggested. No one will judge or even comment on the ideas at this point.

3. Then we will go through all the ideas and decide which ones we *all* thing might work. It is important that everyone agree on the solutions we pick. If we do not find any solutions, it means we either didn't define the problem well enough or did not look hard enough for possible answers. If so, we will go back to step number one and try again. If we get the problem defined well and everyone's needs stated, we will be much more likely to find some creative workable solutions which everyone will accept, if not like.

4. We will then decide which solution we all think is the best possible for all of us. We may combine two or more ideas to come up with a solution that is better than any one alone would have been. It is very important to check with every single person in the group to make sure the solution is okay with each of them and decide together.

5. When we have selected a possible solution, then it is time to decide together how we will make it work. This means deciding who will do what, and when, and how, and where we will get the materials needed to carry out the plan. At this point, we must be sure everyone agrees to do his or her part of what is needed. If someone does not agree, it is important to stop and inquire whether that person really feels okay about the solution. Everyone must agree to the solution (compromise) in order to make it work well; we also need to set times for each part of the solution to begin.

6. The last step is to get the okay of everyone, that each accepts the solution and plans to cooperate with it. Then you can set a time when the group will check back to see how the solution is working. It is important for the secretary to write that all down. All need to decide how the check back will be done.

Most people really do want to help each other when they understand each others feelings and needs. Working on our group problems together is like paths and bridges between each of us. This is a big help in getting to know each other better. It also helps us learn to respect and like each other. We can get together to work on problems and opportunities in ways which are better than any of us can do alone. This is called *problem solving*. We will be doing it together when ever we can.

INTERACTION ACTIVITIES

Illustrated Problem Solving

Build a story around the problem solving steps by illustrating each one with a characteristic of nature. For example:

1. Listening for the problem— *an elephant* with her big ears

2. Brainstorming for ideas—*a rainstorm* showering down raindrops.

3. Evaluating ideas—*a giraffe* with long neck to stretch out to check out all ideas.

4. Picking a solution—*a monkey* picking bananas.

5. Implementing the plan—*an octopus* with her many arms (one arm is "who", one is "where", one is "when", "how", etc.

6. Checking to see if the plan is working—*an owl* with her big eyes.

Draw or cut out pictures to visually communicate each point. Have fun being creative.

✛ ✛ ✛ ✛

Solve That Problem

Write the steps of problem solving so all can see (see description at beginning of chapter) and leave them posted. Invite group members to share or write down problems they would like to solve, and choose two or three which interest the entire group. Invite the owner of each problem to select persons to role play the people who are involved in the problem situation. have her instruct them as to their roles. Then facilitate as they work through the problem solving steps. Discuss later the results according to how well each solution worked.

✛ ✛ ✛ ✛

"It's Brainstorming Time!"

Materials: Drawing pad and marker

Invite the participants to sit in a circle and write a starter phrase on the scratch pad. Use one of the following or your own idea:

What is…

Imagine that…

What if we could…

Then open it up to whatever comes from the group in pure brainstorming. Nothing is too zany or looney. Write down each response and do not evaluate or judge any contribution. Suggest various categories and prime the pump with some of your own if the start is slow. For example:

What if…

Color: Trees were purple, telephone poles were pink, etc.

Time: School started at 8:00 p.m., getting up at midnight, etc.

National: The Rocky Mountains went flat, California changed to New York, etc.

Sound: Thunder sounded like a marching band, sirens played the Star Spangled Banner, school bells played the Mickey Mouse song, etc.

Discuss some of the funny images created by these brainstorms. Guide the discussion into the idea that brainstorming means saying whatever comes into my head and not judging or evaluating my own or anyone else's idea whether realistic or not.

Variation: Invite the participants to make pictures of some of their favorite brainstorms and post them or take them home as reminders.

Problem Solving Practice

Have persons divide into groups of four or five and select a secretary for each group. Provide newsprint and markers for all groups and ask them to record every idea generated by the group. Instruct them not to criticize or evaluate during the brainstorming session, to accept even the far-fetched ideas, and to work for a large number of ideas. Give them a drawing to represent brainstorming such as a raincloud showering down drops.

Now, introduce a situation such as:

1. You have been cast ashore on a desert island with nothing but a belt. What can you do to help stay alive with the belt?

2. You are the owner of a paper cup factory, and somehow 10,000 cups are made without bottoms. What can be done to use these bottomless cups?

Give the group time to generate ideas, then call them back together and share all ideas. If desired, have an evaluation stage, and reach consensus on the five most useful ideas. Discuss problem solving as a tool to deal with everyday situations.

Variation: Have a contest between groups to see which one can generate the most ideas, but do not stress winning and losing.

Let's Find Out!

Separate the group into teams of three or five participants. Make paper, scotch tape, glue, stapler, and two or three yardsticks available for all to use.

Give each group the following problem: "Using the six-stop method of problem solving, plan and prepare a method to achieve a composite description of your group including as many statistics as you can and want to." Display on the wall or otherwise post the six-step problem solving method where everyone can see and a sample of possible facts which the group could compile such as:

1. Composite height

2. Composite weight

3. Composite years in school

4. Composite number of relatives living within a twenty-five mile radius

(add any others and allow groups to select, add, and subtract)

Coach the groups to use the no-lose problem solving approach to secure their own special "group profile". As leader, coach with positive reinforcements and encourage process more than content. Do not do it for them; encourage them!

When all groups have had sufficient time, ask for a report on the content, the process, and their feelings about working together in this way. Help participants to recap the six steps as you saw them being utilized.

Let's Plan

Introduce to the group the possibility of taking a trip together. Help them settle on the important questions to problem solve, such as what kind of a trip, where and when to go, what to do, etc. Brainstorm on each issue. When many ideas have been generated, end the brainstorming session and evaluate the ideas. Reach consensus and make plans to implement the trip if feasible. Discuss the problem solving process. How well did it work for group planning?

Variation: Help the group use the problem solving steps to solve current group questions such as what to do for the next ten minutes, what to do next week, or what to do if some people finish an activity before others.

Act Out The Problem

Divide into groups of not more than five persons. Give a task to each group and allow them to prepare a drama enacting how they would solve the problem and complete the task. Discuss the problem solving method of:

1. Defining the problem
2. Brainstorming ideas
3. Evaluating ideas
4. Choosing an idea
5. Implementing the idea
6. Checking back to see that it is working

Suggest that if they do not have what they need for the drama, they are free to invent the needed materials.

Possible scenes:

1. Your group must get across a wide, rushing river and land all of its members safely on the other side. Only one person in the group can swim.

2. Your group is besieged by wild and hungry animals and you must find safety for all. There is a cabin on top a hill, but one of your persons has broken her leg.

3. Think of other possible scenes for the dramas.

✝ ✝ ✝ ✝

How We Worked It Out

Let each participant be either a person-character or an animal. Divide speaking lines as desired. If desirable, use puppets to act out the characters.

Narrator: This is today, and the time is now. The place is the great jungle of life, and the characters are you and me. The vines are thick and the trees are high; the paths are overgrown, and we don't know which way to go. We only know one thing; we have a problem. The problem is how to find our way. We are friends, and we care about one another. What shall we do?

(Enter the elephants)

Elephants: Listen, Listen, Listen! Listen to each other, listen to the trees, the birds, the wind. If you listen, you will find out much. This is the first step of problem solving.

Person 1: Wow, did you see that! What did they mean "listen"? I'm scared, and I want to get some place where the path is clearer and I can see where I'm going.

Person 2: You do? I think it's kind of fun to be here even though it's scary too.

Person 3: I'm tired and hungry, and I just want to rest and get something to eat.

Person 1: Well, they said to listen and what I heard was that you like it here, you are tired and hungry and (points to self) I want a clear path. Right?

Persons 1 and 2: RIGHT!

Person 2: It's starting to rain, at least that should cool us off a little and maybe we'll get some ideas about what we can do.

(Enter the rainstormers; they are raindrops who rustle around rubbing the palms of their hands together to simulate rain. They represent "brainstorming", the second step in the problem solving process.)

Person 1: Let's brainstorm this rainstorm: and for every rumble of thunder we can try to come up with an idea about what to do.

Person 3: I'll write them all down in my little notebook I carry.

Person 2: Well, we could pick some fruit off the trees to eat since we're hungry.

Person 3: Yes, and we could sit down and just look around at everything that's here.

Person 1: We could scout around for paths to see which ones are clearest and get an idea of where they go.

Person 2: We could sing a song to cheer ourselves up a little.

Person 1: We could do some exercises to limber up.

Person 3: And we could climb a tree to look around and see where we are. Hey…wait a minute… I'm not getting these all down.

Person 2: We could all go separate directions to see what we can find.

Person 1: And we could…I can't think of any more.

Person 3: I'm glad, because I'm almost out of paper.

Person 1: The storm's over anyhow…look at those giraffes.

(Enter the giraffes, weaving their heads around atop their long necks.)

Giraffes: Look! Listen! Evaluate your ideas! Look! Listen! Evaluate! This is the third step Eeval-luuaate!

Person 2: Evaluate? What's that? What are those funny giraffes talking about?

Person 3: EEE-value-ate. Maybe it's like something to eat or maybe it's the number "eight". Sounds like that.

Person 1: No it's different. I know 'cause I heard my mom say that word once, but I don't remember what it means.

Person 2: Mrs. Giraffe, what does "evaluate" mean?

Giraffe 1: (in deep voice) Why, my girl, it means to decide whether you think something is okay or not okay, whether it's good or bad, You've got a lot of ideas there. Now it's time to "evaluate" them.

Giraffe 2: And if any one of you thinks an ideas **isn't** okay, then it just isn't okay for your group. That's part of problem solving.

Person 1: This jungle sure has a lot of "steps" and animals to help us out. First the elephants, then the rainstormers, then these giraffes, and now…

Person 2: And NOW, look at those monkeys!

(Enter the monkeys.)

Monkeys: Pickee, Pickee, Pickee. When you've evaluated, then you can pick, and if you pick together and if you agree, you'll work together well and find the best way for YOU. Picking and choosing is the fourth step.

Person 3: I think she's right. Let's evaluate and pick together what to do. Then we'll all feel okay about it, and we'll all be trying to do what's best for all of us.

Persons 1 and 2: Okay with me!

Person 3: I'll read the list of ideas and we can all say "yes" or "no". Pick fruit to eat (everyone Yes!). Sit down and look around at everything (1 and 2 say No, 3 says Yes). I guess I can wait on that since you guys don't want to now. (reads on) Scout for

paths to see what's clear and where to go.

Everyone: Yes!

Person 2: But let's do it together.

Person 3: Then there was "sing a song to cheer ourselves up, and do some exercises".

Persons 1 and 2: No! We've got more important things to do.

Person 3: What about climbing a tree to look around? I don't think it's a good idea, because the tall trees don't have any low branches to climb on. The last idea was to all go separate ways to see what we can find.

Person 1: I want to stay together for now.

Person 3: Well, we all agreed, then, to pick some fruit and then scout together?

(Enter octopus. Have a few persons stand behind each other waving their arms as if they are one person.)

Person 2: Hey, look at that octopus over there. I didn't know we were near an ocean.

Person 1: She seems to be saying something. Can you hear what it is?

Octopus: I have so many arms I can carry out my plans by myself. You must **work together** to solve you problems. This is the fifth step of problem solving.

Person 3: Okay, I guess we're supposed to work together according to this crazy jungle.

Person 1: I'll get the fruit.

Person 2: I'll help peel it.

Person 3: And I'll help eat it! Then we can scout together.

(Enter the owls.)

Owl: Look and watch! Use your eyes. See how your plan is working. If you see it working well, you will know to continue. If you see a need to change, then you'll plan some more. This is the last step of your problem solving. You have learned your lesson well.

Elephant: Listen, listen, listen, decide what your problem is.

Rainstormers: Brainstorm all your ideas and solutions!

Giraffes: Evaluate, evaluate, see what is best for all.

Monkeys: Pick and choose, pick and choose, pick only the ideas everyone okays.

Octopus: Work together to put your plan in action.

Owl: Watch and see, watch and see if your plan is working.

Narrator: The place is the great jungle of life, but the elephants, the rainstormers, the monkeys, the octopus, and the owls have gone. We will remember the steps they taught us and work together to solve all our problems.

THE END

✦ ✦ ✦ ✦

Kitchen Problems And Opportunities

Decide on a group project for the kitchen such as making a pizza. Provide a variety of toppings and let group members solve the problem of dividing them so that everyone gets what she wants on her part of the pizza. Discuss problem solving as a tool for making everyday decisions. The kitchen makes an ideal lab for practice in problem solving and is adaptable to as large or as small a project as is feasible for the group to undertake. The reinforcement of eaten together the results of the group is an added "plus".

✦ ✦ ✦ ✦

Apple Fun

Provide as many variations of apples as can be found with no less than one whole apple for each participant.

Depending on the age of the participants, explain, or ask them to research and explain about each apple variety (e.g. color, texture, taste, uses, where grown, any special information).

Share the apple information in a circle and then enter into a problem solving or decision-making process to decide what to do with the apples. Be prepared for a variety of uses including baking, eating raw, giving away, making centerpieces, etc. Be sure that the brainstorm segment is fully completed so that all possible ideas from the group are aired. As leader, function as one of the group during evaluation; you have the same privilege of veto as all others, however, this is a great opportunity to be flexible and to stretch your thinking as to what is okay and useful. (Some questions to ask yourself: does everyone have to do the same activity? Why? Is it okay if someone wants to sit and watch? Is it okay for someone to think of and do something you didn't even consider as a possibility? Do you trust yourself? Your group? What are your needs in this situation?)

When the problem solving is complete and implementation is underway, some may be waiting for cooking processes to take place, others may be through with their activities (it doesn't take long to eat a raw apple!).

Here is a short "apple" sharing variety. Ask all participants to sit in a circle and to choose an apple variety they would like to be (if they were apples). Then invite the participants, one by one, to enter the center of the circle and describe themselves in apple language (e.g. I am yellow and golden, not quite ripe, still hanging on the branch of my parent tree in a huge orchard on the hillside in Washington, etc.). When all have taken center stage, allow time for group discussion and sharing.

✦ ✦ ✦ ✦

Gorp Goop: An Exercise In Individual Or Group Problem Solving

Gorp is a fun mixture of many kinds of good nourishing foods. It is usually packed into plastic bags and is fun to eat just about any time except right before a meal!

Possible ingredients: raisins, bits of hard cheese, corn chips, sesame seeds, granola, dates, wheat germ, pretzels, Cheerios, sunflower seeds, Wheat Chex, Rice Chex, peanuts, walnuts, other nuts, other dry cereal, coconut, any kind of dried fruit.

Provide or let the group shop with you for a variety of ingredients to be used for your Gorp. Place each ingredient in a container on a large table or work area.

Give a plastic bag to each participant and invite her to go through the entire problem solving process for herself in deciding and producing her own Gorp. This is a form of short-range goal-setting and completion; it is simple and fun for any age child.

Have a Gorp party and discuss how each person made her choices and completed the process.

ARTS AND CRAFTS

Blown Eggs

As an exercise in problem solving, brainstorm how to remove the insides from a raw egg shell without breaking the shell. Follow the steps of problem solving, and try out many of the brainstormed ideas to evaluate their effectiveness. If the group ends up with any whole shells with insides drained out, paint them with acrylic paint, or drip melted wax on their surface and dye the eggs.

✛ ✛ ✛ ✛

Problem Solving Mobiles

Materials: Sticks, wires, branches, dowels
                    or coat hangers
                Glue and tape
                Scissors
                All kinds of "stuff" and "junk"
                    to hang

Invite the participants to create mobiles to hang however and wherever they like. Encourage problem solving for any aspect of the process from gathering the supplies to making the components of their mobiles representative of the six-step process. This a free wheeling activity which can give lots of space for individual differences, preferences, capabilities, and timing.

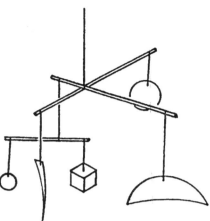

Display the mobiles and give each creator a chance to explain her production. If all are using the six steps as content for their mobiles, this gives an unusually good opportunity to make a presentation to another group through a show, display, or other presentation. Allow plenty of time and scope for gathering the "stuff".

✛ ✛ ✛ ✛

Blottos

Materials: Paper
                Paint
                Scissors
                Paste

Cut a number of paper squares and rectangles of various sizes. Ask each person to choose a piece of paper and crease it in the middle so that later it can be folded easily. Invite her to sprinkle a few drops of paint on one side of the crease, fold the paper on the creased line with the paint inside, and press. This cause the paint to be squeezed into a variety of interesting shapes. Open the paper to see the surprising results. Brainstorm with the group what each blotto resembles. Reach consensus, and title each picture.

Variation: Invite dyads, tryads, or other small groups to form and use the problem solving steps to title the blottos.

✛ ✛ ✛ ✛

Personal Problem Solving: "How I Will Make My Own Terrarium"

Post the six steps of problem solving and encourage each person to consider, brainstorm evaluate, select her own choices, implement them, and decide when to check back for results.

Materials: Glass jar with removable lids
(one for each participant)
Soil and crushed charcoal
Gravel
Crushed rock
Plants (various types)
Shells
Rock, figures, other objects

Invite each person to choose a jar. Explain and demonstrate placing a layer of charcoal to keep the soil fresh-smelling, gravel for drainage, and soil of 1½ to 2 inches thick. Explain and demonstrate the placing of plants by scooping out soil to make holes for roots, placing plants in the holes, and pressing soil gently around the roots and sprinkling with water. Accessories are to be offered without demonstration.

Explain the needs of a terrarium for growth to occur: cover, place where there is bright light without hot sun, rotate for balanced growth. If the lid is kept on, watering is not necessary.

After demonstrating, encourage each participant to work with the problem solving model of decision-making to prepare her own terrarium. Encourage and accept all efforts.

Variation: Use a two quart milk carton, plant as usual, cut rectangles on each side, cover with plastic sheets (hard), water and close up.

✣ ✣ ✣ ✣

Problem Solving Wind Chimes

Materials: Clay
Rolling pin
Waxed paper
Knitting needle
Tempera paints
Dowel rod or other support piece
Brushes
Shellac
Newspapers
Strong twine or leather thongs

Review the steps of problem solving in order, and invite each participant to write down a simple symbol she likes for each step (e.g. a jagged and uneven circle for the problem; a many-sided form for the brainstorming; a star for the evaluation; a triangle for the selection, etc.).

Invite each participant to make a six-part wind chime with each problem solving symbol as one of the parts. The process for making the parts is as follows:

1. Roll thick clay slabs onto waxed paper somewhat like pie dough.

2. Cut the symbols from the clay.

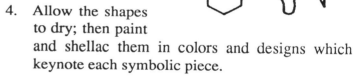

3. Make a hole through each shape with a knitting needle.

4. Allow the shapes to dry; then paint and shellac them in colors and designs which keynote each symbolic piece.

5. Connect the shapes by stringing the twine or thong through each one. Tie a knot beneath each piece and attach the twine or thong to the support piece (dowel rod, strong twig, etc.). Hang in the wind and listen to the sound of your own "Problem Solving Wind Chime".

The entire process is loaded with opportunities to talk about problem solving, to facilitate in mini-problem solving situations, and to enjoy making something beautiful.

Variation: For older children, encourage a string of symbolic symbols for each problem solving step.

✣ ✣ ✣ ✣

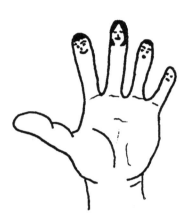

Problem Solving Puppets

There are many puppets possibilities so take your pick from the following or your own ideas and collect the necessary materials:

Popsicle-stick puppets

Spoon puppets (convex side is face)

Box puppets (cereal or cracker)

Finger puppets (decorate fingers as faces)

Hand puppets (closed fist with thumb for lower lip and chin; decorate as a face)

Foot puppets (each toe is a person, bottoms up)

Paper plates and sticks

Fruits and vegetables dressed up

Paper sack puppets

The puppets can be dressed up and trimmed with all kinds of materials including fabric scraps, fluffy cotton balls, buttons, ribbon, yarn and string, seeds or pasta shapes, pipe cleaners, feathers, straws, or toothpicks, wire, paper clips, rubber bands, etc.

Invite each participant to create her puppet family or individual. Then prepare a show incorporating the six steps of problem solving with each individual doing her own act or part of the act. Use problem solving to prepare the show and then present it for another group—possibly parents!

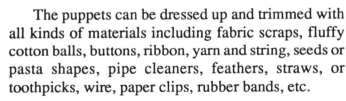

✛   ✛   ✛   ✛

Brainstorm-A-Brick

Materials: Bricks and cement blocks of
various shapes and sizes
Enamel paint
Glue
Paper scraps, pictures, felt, fabric
Scissors
Nick-knacks such as buttons,
feathers, pipe cleaners, beads,
etc.

Place all the bricks and cement blocks on newspaper and make a circle around them to do group decision-making (problem solving) before beginning projects.

1. Define the problem or decision to be made (e.g. we have fifteen bricks and eight participants—how to distribute them or we have enough for all, but no ideas of what to use them for).

2. Brainstorm solutions for the defined problem or decision. Make sure that someone is writing down all suggested solutions and that no one is making evaluations at this time.

3. Evaluate the brainstormed ideas and identify the solutions or decisions which are agreeable to everyone.

4. Choose the most feasible solutions which are agreeable to all.

5. Decide how to put the plans into motion (implement).

6. Decide when and how to check out for continuing satisfaction and need-meeting.

Note to group leaders: If participants do not come up with ideas for brick use, prime the pump with some of these ideas: decorate for bookend, use with boards for bookcase (might be a group project for the meeting place). Decorate for a doorstop, decorate the ones with holes for pencil holders or private mail boxes. Use materials listed for decorating.

Pick-A-Stick

Invite participants to sit in a circle for problem solving activity to prepare for selecting, preparing, decorating and showing their own personal sticks. A stick is good for lots of things—to lean on, to take on a walk, to bat an old tin can around with, to talk to, just to stand in a corner to remind you of problem solving!

Invite the participants to consider where and how to locate proper "sticks" for the activity. Use this as a basic problem solving model:

1. Define problem—how and where can we get good-sized sticks for each member of the group.

2. Brainstorm for ideas; let them fly and record all. No evaluation now.

3. Evaluate every idea as a group. Identify the ones seen as "okay" by all.

4. Choose the most feasible idea.

5. Figure out who will do what and when and how.

6. Set a time for checking out whether the plan is working.

When every person has a stick (the problem is solved), invite the participants to decorate their sticks to represent the problem solving steps. Encourage uses of color, carving, glued-on objects, etc. Have a Stick Show and invite each participant to explain her stick.

INDIVIDUAL CENTERS

Problem Solving Opportunities

1. Post the steps for problem solving with pictures to illustrate each of the various steps. See "Illustrated Problem Solving" page 111 for pictorial suggestions.

2. Present various "opportunities" which can be "solved" through the problem solving process such as:

    A. A Vacation—you want to go on a vacation but don't have any ideas about where to go, how long it would take, how much money it would cost, etc.

    B. A Project—you want to build something but don't have ideas of what is possible with your skills and your resources.

3. Provide information which an individual can use to get brainstorming ideas. For example:

    A. A vacation—have on hand travel magazines, road atlas, cost information, etc.

    B. A Project—supply store catalogues which have possible items to buy and build and mail order catalogues with kits to assemble, etc.

4. Encourage persons to follow the problem solving steps of identifying the problem, brainstorming ideas, evaluating, picking a solution, and if feasible, implementing the solution and checking to see if the plan is working. Think of other "problems" which individuals could work through with the problem solving steps.

✣ ✣ ✣ ✣

Personal Goal Setting

To help group members pinpoint areas in their lives they might want to improve, ask them to fill out #1 *Define Problem (or Opportunity)* (see Personal Goal Setting posters at end of chapter), checking the appropriate column for each item. The chart covers many aspects of group members' lives, some of which will be very important to them while others will not be important. Encourage them to fill in the blanks at the bottom of #1 with other items of interest to them. Take time to share about the items they listed in the "Okay" column.

Ask them to look at their "Want to Improve" column and to choose the five items they most want to change. These five can be written in *Select Your Goals*.

Invite group members to circle one of these five that they would like to work on with another person.

The activity may continue as an individual exercise

but works well to be done in pairs from step three to seven. Divide the group into dyads and ask each person to describe the goal he has circled, where he is with it now, and where he wants to go with it. The pair may now take turns brainstorming for each other's goals. Ask them to write down all these ideas in #2 *Brainstorm for Ideas on How to Achieve Your Goals*. It is *very* important that they do not evaluate the idea at this time, but simply write them all down.

When brainstorming is done, invite both partners to evaluate all the ideas by checking "okay" in #3 *Evaluate Brainstorming Ideas* for all the ideas that might possibly work, and "not okay" for those that will not work.

Each person may then choose one solution to try, and write it in #4 *Design Your Action Plan*. Encourage them after the session to follow steps #5 *Put Your Plan into Action*, and #6 *Check the Outcome*. They may report to the group at a later time on the process they have made toward achieving their goals.

BOOKS

Picture Books

Alexander, Martha G., **Sabrina**.
Barton, Byron, **Where's Al?**
Bottner, Barbara, **Mean Maxine**.
Dickinson, Mary, **Alex's Bed**.
Lionni, Leo, **Swimmy**.

Fiction Books

Alexander, Martha G., **Move Over, Twerp**.
Bonsall, Crosby Newell, **The Case Of The Double Cross**.
Carris, Joan Davenport, **When The Boys Ran The House**.
Chapman, Caro, **Herbie's Troubles**.
Cleary, Beverly B., **Henry And The Clubhouse**.
Cleary, Beverly B., **Henry And The Paper Route**.
Flournoy, Valerie, **The Twins Strike Back**.
Hoban, Russell Cowell, **A Bargain For Frances**.
Inkiow, Dimiter, **Me And Clara And Casimer The Cat**.
Mauser, Pat Rhoads, **How I Found Myself At The Fair**.
McDonnell, Christine, **Don't Be Made, Ivy**.
Morey, Walter, **Home Is The North**.
Peck, Robert Newton, **A Day No Pigs Would Die**.
Pfeffer, Susan Beth, **What Do You Do When Your Mouth Won't Open**.
Quigley, Lillian Fox, **The Blind Men And The Elephant**.
Robertson, Keith, **Henry Reed's Baby-sitting Service**.
Waber, Bernard, **Ira Sleeps Over**.
Wright, Betty Ryan, **I Like Being Alone**.

Personal Goal Setting

1. Define Problem (or Opportunity)

RATE THE ITEMS

	Okay	Want to Improve	Not Important
Relationship with parents			
Singing			
Playing Games			
Keeping My Room			
Being Liked			
Being a Good Sport			
Posture			
Sports			
Weight			
Playing Music			
How I Dress			
Hair Care			
Liking Myself			
Talking to Friends			
Being a Leader			
Relating to Brothers and Sisters			
Being Friendly			
Helping Others			
Making Good Grades			
Making Friends			
Complexion			
Art			
What I Eat			
How I Look			
Having Friends			
_____			
_____			
_____			

SELECT YOUR GOALS (Choose from the middle column above)

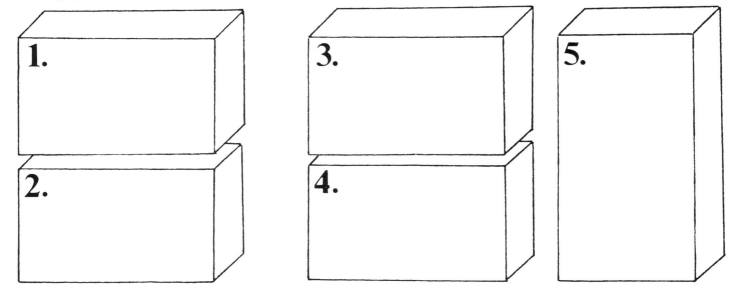

1.

2.

3.

4.

5.

2. Brainstorm for Ideas on How to Achieve Your Goals

3. Evaluate Brainstorming Ideas

Okay   Not Okay

_____   _____   _____

_____   _____   _____

_____   _____   _____

_____   _____   _____

_____   _____   _____

_____   _____   _____

_____   _____   _____

_____   _____   _____

_____   _____   _____

_____   _____   _____

_____   _____   _____

4. Design Your Action Plan

What? _____

Where? _____

When? _____

How? _____

5. Put Your Plan into Action

6. Check the Outcome

CHAPTER 9

Helping And Cooperation

INTRODUCTION OF CONCEPT

Helping and cooperation are such common terms that we often overlook the skills involved. But helping and cooperation deserve our special attention. Both of these are strong components of relationship.

Helping

Whenever we *help* someone do something that he or she could and might prefer to do alone, we deny that person the opportunity of personal achievement. It is appropriate to offer assistance, but we must then be prepared to receive in good will the response of acceptance or rejection. If the response is positive and help is given, the helper takes responsibility only for helping, not for the outcome of the task. The helper allows the other person to "own" the success or failure of the task.

Cooperation

Cooperation, however, implies that the recipient offers and receives investment from the cooperator in the planning and implementation of the task. "Cooperation" is thus a more involved kind of participation, and a more potent relationship builder. In cooperation, a partnership of task commitment is shared and ownership of success or failure is joint.

As we help and cooperate with one another, we promote unity, we affirm the importance of persons as being worth helping, and we demonstrate that working together can bring results which exceed individual potential. These are all strong components of relationship strength.

The helper is encouraged by helping. The receiver sees the job completed, thus realizing the value of assistance. Cooperators enjoy the synergy of uniting themselves toward a common goal. Self esteem, energy, and group cohesiveness are promoted.

Again, the relationships are affirmed!

INTRODUCTION TO PARTICIPANTS

There are times when each of us needs help. There are also times when each of us can give help.

If we are always the person giving help, we may not be thinking enough about how we could get along better ourselves with a little help from someone else.

If we are always the one receiving help, we may be overlooking the ways in which we could help someone else.

If my house needs to be painted or repaired, my neighbors might like to help me if I asked them. Then, in return, I can be willing to help when they have a project. In the classroom, one of you may be able to do math quite easily and could help someone who finds math difficult. This does not mean doing it for the other person, but rather explaining *how* to do it and helping the other person along toward success. That person may be able to help you with art or something that is hard for you. Perhaps someone entirely different will be the one to help you. If we pass on to others the help we receive, we will all be more likely to get help when we need it.

"You can ask for what you need" is a motto for all of us. We may not always be able to receive *all* that we need or deliver *all* that others need. We can, however, care about each other and cooperate in ways to get our needs met more often than when we try to do it all alone.

We will be doing some special activities to help us think more about helping and cooperation as well as other things we have learned. In our times together and at home, helping and cooperation can be a fun and worthwhile way of living with each other.

INTERACTION ACTIVITIES

Three Legged Race

Divide the group into pairs and give each a length of cloth to use in tying their inside legs together. Have a race with the teams tied in this way—the importance of cooperation becomes evident.

Variation: Tie persons together at the waists or arms and have them try a relay or obstacle course.

"Handy" Cooperation

Divide the group into twos (or dyads) facing one another. Ask them to match the palms of their right hands at arm's length, close their eyes, and gently press palm to palm. With eyes still closed, ask them to place both hands at their sides, and both persons turn around in place four times. Then, still with eyes closed, ask them to match right palms again in the original position.

The exercise opens the door for one-to-one cooperation. Discuss the experience in twos and as a group to share the variety of reactions.

The "Back-Up" Game

Invite the participants to find a partner to form a dyad. Have partners sit back-to-back with knees bent and feet drawn up toward the body. Invite partners to link their arms at the elbow and then stand up together. This requires cooperation.

Invite dyads to join another dyad to make a foursome and again stand up together. This requires *more* cooperation! Add as many as is feasible and discuss what is required to successfully complete the "standup". Use the experience as a take-off point for discussion of cooperation and skills. Encourage, reinforce, listen, and allow time for sharing.

Variation: A venturesome group may want to try for a "mass standup". To do so, instruct the participants to sit close to one another, wedged firmly together. Let them all stand at the count of three. If everyone gets up, a major feat of cooperation had been achieved.

Balloon Toss-Up

Materials: At least as many balloons as participants—blown up and tied

The object of the game is to keep all the balloons off the ground by blowing, patting, lifting, nudging,

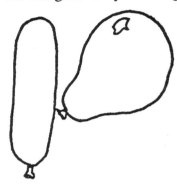

tossing, or whatever seems to work best. Invite the participants to work together to keep all the balloons in the air for a given period of time. This is a fun activity which gets everyone involved and serves as an excellent warm-up.

Tangled Knots

Invite the participants to form a circle, stretching both hands outward toward the center. Instruct everyone to clasp hands with two people across the circle from him and to hand on (be sure that no one has both hands clasped with the same individual and that no one is clasping the hand of his next door neighbor in the circle).

The result of the hand clasping is an enormous knot. The object is to cooperate as a group to unravel the knot which can be done and will result in one large circle or two interconnected ones. Participants may step over or under hands but are not to let go until the knot is untangled.

The nature of the exercise pulls in all loners and "outsiders" into full participation and is an experience in group helping. Discussion can focus around a number of facets including:

1. Have each person share his reaction to the problem.

2. Note how leadership was taken or given and compare this to other leadership patterns.

3. Compare this physical tangle to other life situations.

4. Consider what was required to untangle the group. What were barriers? What were helps?

A Cooperative "Fuzzy" Circle

Materials: Cotton balls, fringe balls, or a large fuzzy ball of brightly colored yarn
"Eyes" available at craft shops
Glue

Invite the participants to sit in a circle. Holding the ball of yarn, share from personal experience two or three recent instances of helping and cooperation which were especially meaningful to you and tell why. Then address another participant of your choice with a starter such as "_____, I like it when you... (smile at me, help with cleanup, etc.)". Deliver the ball of yarn while holding onto one end of the thread and invite the receiver to give a "fuzzy" and send the ball of yarn on to another person who then does the same until all have received and given. NOTE: Avoid saying "I like *you* when ..." this is conditional acceptance and implies that I do *not* accept you at other times. Avoid "It makes me..." This lays power and/or guilt onto the recipient and may be negative in its effect. Other useful starters:

"When you help by _____, I feel happy."

"I appreciate it when you... because..."

If cotton balls or fuzzies are to be used, the project can involve decorating them which is often very useful in that the participants invest some of themselves in the objects they will then give away. The exchanges are then made with appropriate "starters" and everyone gives and receives. If possible, overextend the number of "fuzzies" so that all may receive and give with a sense of "plenty" rather than of closed-endedness or limitation.

✛ ✛ ✛ ✛

The "Jacket" Game

Invite one participant to be "it". "It" will act as though he has no knowledge about what a jacket is for or how to put it on. The other participants are to "explain", without touching, how to put on the jacket. Encourage the use of "I" messages, influencing statements, and positive reinforcement as the person begins to "catch on". Instruct "it" that he is to behave as if he really does not know, but is hearing about jackets for the first time from the group. The group will experience a need for cooperation through trying to instruct and help him. When the jacket is finally "on", discuss the

exercise including what was an was not helpful to the person being "it".

✛ ✛ ✛ ✛

Cooperation And Helping Wheel

Form a circle with the participants and brainstorm together a long list of friendly, helpful acts and ways to be cooperative. When the brainstorm is fully completed, invite the participants to evaluate which acts they would most appreciate receiving.  Write each of these on a separate slip of paper, fold, and number each so that the papers correspond to a number on the "cooperation and helping wheel" described and pictured here.

Using a wheel similar to the picture with numbered wedges and an arrow of tagboard fastened by a paper fastener, invite the participants to spin the arrow to a number, match up the numbered paper, and role play the helping and cooperation act described. Coach and encourage them to involve each other in the role plays and to reinforce one another for trying. These may be new experiences for many in the group. They will learn from each other new ways of helping if the atmosphere is accepting, friendly, and non-judgmental. Invite them to share their feelings and experiences concerning the role plays.

Extend the activity further if desired by inviting each participant to choose one friendly, helpful act he would like to do outside the group in a real-life situation. Designate group time at a later date for sharing experiences.

Possible role play brainstorms:

1. Smile at someone

2. Help someone clean up a mess

3. Sit beside someone new

4. Talk to someone I don't know well

5. Make something for a member of my family or this group

6. Eat snacks or lunch with someone who is alone

7. Listen to a friend talk about what he wants or needs

8. Do an errand for someone

9. Loan something to someone

✟ ✟ ✟ ✟

"I'd Like To Know..."

Designate a box to be used for questions by placing a slot in the top where written questions may be deposited. Invite group members to write out questions about which they want to know more and place them in the box. From time to time, answer the questions which have been deposited. Encourage discussion and sharing; treat each inquiry with respect. Model helping and cooperation in answering questions.

✟ ✟ ✟ ✟

Blind Risk

Materials: Blindfolds for one half the members of participants
Blockade materials

Invite the participants to create an obstacle course as complex as feasible within the given space including objects placed upside down, out of usual order, and arranged in various ways which would be confusing to a sightless person (use chairs, desks, etc.).

Ask the participants to divide themselves into partners either by numbering off or by volunteer arrangement. One of the persons in each pair will then put on a blindfold and allow his partner to take him through the obstacle course four times as follows:

1. A blindfolded, B leads him through and back using both speech and touch.

2. A blindfolded, B leads him through and back using *ONLY* speech for guidance.

3. B blindfolded, A leads him through and back using both speech and touch.

4. B blindfolded, A leads him through and back using both *ONLY* for guidance.

Before and during the exercise, coach, encourage and reinforce responsibility and trust of one another. After the activity has been finished by all, discuss, including the following as appropriate:

1. What feelings did you experience while blindfolded? As leader?

2. Which way of being led did you prefer? Which required the most cooperation and trust?

3. What was helpful to you? Describe for the group.

4. What was difficult for you? Describe.

5. What did you learn from this experience?

✟ ✟ ✟ ✟

Co-Op Ice Cream

A group can learn to work together effectively in cooperative fashion when presented with the necessity or the opportunity to experience a built-in pleasant reward. Freezing ice cream with an old-fashioned crank freezer provides this kind of necessity and reward.

Decisions about the ice cream recipe and supplies can be problem-solved by the six steps (see Chapter 8). When the freezer is ready to have the crank turned, invite all participants to do their part in a cooperative endeavor to keep the crank turning until the ice cream is frozen. They will then enjoy the cooperative experience of serving, eating, and cleaning up from their activity.

✟ ✟ ✟ ✟

Having A Ball

Invite the participants to join in the exercise which will be done according to the following rules:

1. The person who is holding the ball is the only one who may speak and he must continue to speak while holding the ball.

2. Anyone may attempt to secure the ball by non-verbal communication but not through force.

3. The person who holds the ball may release it to someone who signals for it, or may choose to keep it.

4. If the ball is released to another individual, he may then talk. The same rules for securing, releasing, and talking are in force.

Introduce a topic for the group to discuss and give the ball to someone in the group who will then proceed by the above rules. Allow the natural course of events to occur, ending the discussion after a short time of interaction.

Invite the participants to discuss their feelings and observations in attempting to gain the ball, hold it, or observe what occurred. Take note of communication patterns which were observed, the use of power, and any struggles which surround its possession. Note also cooperation and its effects in the group (a power struggle can be initiated by placing the ball in the center of the group at the beginning rather than handing it to an individual).

Variation: Have two balls circulating within the group so that two participants will be talking. Use a string ball, unwinding it as it is passed from person to person, making visual patterns of communication.

Lifesaver Relay

Give each participant a toothpick and divide into two teams of equal number. The object of the game is to pass lifesavers (the number to be determined by the leader) from one person to another by toothpicks held in each participant's mouth  in relay style until all the lifesavers are at the end of the line. The first team to complete the "lifesaver pass" has won the cooperation award.

Invite the group to discuss what they think promoted and what hindered group cooperation. If desired, use a stop watch and allow each team to do the pass again while being timed. Invite the non-participant group to encourage, reinforce, and cheer them on so that total group cooperation is encouraged. Reverse the process.

Variation: Smaller children can do this relay by holding the toothpick in their hands to pass the lifesavers.

Cooperative Review Skits

Invite each person or team of persons to assume responsibility for preparing and presenting a skit to illustrate one of the chapter lessons in this book. Give coaching as desired and needed. Some possible ideas for subject designation might include drawing out of a hat; selecting a balloon from nine balloons, each of

which has a subject written on a piece of paper inside; or using the six steps of problem-solving (see Chapter 8) to decide who does what.

Shoe Smorgasbord

Materials: Shoe
Slips of paper with instructions
Table or tray with a variety of foods

In an old shoe or other container, put slips of paper with instructions on them for carrying out a simple behavioral goal such as "Give an 'I' message to someone older than you are", or "Eye level with someone smaller than you", or "Show three strong feelings and have the group guess from your body language." Each participant will take his turn to draw a message from the shoe, go to the smorgasbord table, do what is requested, and receive his choice of food from the table.

This activity will serve as a cooperative review exercise for a group which has completed the curriculum to this point.

Behavioral Bingo

Materials: Heavy paper
Rulers
Markers (beans, etc.)
List of behavioral goals or lesson topics
Pencils

Let each person design his own bingo card by dividing a square of heavy paper into twenty-five (25) equal-sized boxes, and randomly labeling the squares with behavioral goals (e.g. Active Listening, "I" Messages, Problem Solving, Self Reinforcements, etc.). The center box is marked "Free". When each person has finished labeling and decorating his bingo card, the game begins. When a behavioral goal is called, the persons

| B E H A V I O R A L | | | | |
B	I	N	G	O
Active Listening	"I" Message	Self Reinforce	Problem Solving	Active Reinforce
Problem Solving	Positive Reinforce	Active Listening	"I" Message	Self Reinforce
"I" Message	Self Reinforce	FREE	Positive Reinforce	Problem Solving
Positive Reinforce	Active Listening	"I" Message	Self Reinforce	Active Listening
Self Reinforce	Problem Solving	Positive Reinforce	Active Listening	"I" Message

mark it on their card with some kind of marker (beans, pieces of paper, etc.) and then two people must demonstrate the behavior. The first person to get five markers in a row yells "Bingo" and has won that round. Begin the game again for more practice with the behavioral goals. Use simple prizes if desired.

+ + + +

Word-Wonders

Materials: Paper
             Pencils
             Dictionaries if desired

Invite the participants to form teams of not more than three persons each. Give them a brief period of time (adjust to age level) to find and write down as many words as they can from the key words "HELPING AND COOPERATION". These words are to be written on a blackboard or somewhere in plain sight. The same letters may be used only once in a given word but may be reused for another word. When the time is up, combine results for a grand list without duplicates and give all participants a treat. Ignore competitive aspects and encourage all participative effort.

+ + + +

What Would Happen...?

Materials: Paper and pencils

Invite the participants to form teams of two to four persons or use an acceptable means for team formation. Each team will select a "What would happen if..." statement and will write or prepare to act out as many possible results as time allows. If the groups have chosen to act out what they believe "Would happen if...", give opportunity and time for them to do so. If time permits and all are willing, give opportunity for total group members to add their ideas to each "What would happen if..."

Possible topics:

1. What would happen if everyone had the same color skin?

2. What would happen if no one ever needed to sleep?

3. What would happen if everyone had red hair?

4. What would happen if there were no postal service?

5. What would happen if no one knew how to talk?

6. What would happen if people could read each other's minds?

7. What would happen if it never rained or snowed?

8. What would happen if no one ever broke a law?

9. What would happen if there were no such thing as money?

10. What would happen if school were not required?

Encourage cooperative effort in thinking, listing, and acting out if this is a part of the agreed-upon activity. Suspend all judgment and accept imaginative ideas.

+ + + +

Cooperative Relaxation Exercise

Invite the participants to form a circle, each facing the back of the person next to him. Model a very gentle smoothing of neck and shoulder muscles, gradually becoming more vigorous into a kneading motion, going on to a gentle chop-chop, and gradually reversing the process. Lead the participants in giving this attention to the person in front of them and receiving it from the person behind. Take three or four minutes to complete the process, ending very slowly and gently with the hands resting quietly on the shoulders of the person ahead. Invite the group to turn and lead them in the same process, working on the neck and shoulders of the person on the other side. When the exercise is complete, let the group be quiet for a few moments of contemplation, then open for sharing.

+ + + +

Helping Scenes

Divide into small groups. Set a scene for each group, ask them to decide who will act out each part, and how the scene will end. Give them time to practice and then ask each group to act out their scene for the large group. Discuss the ways persons in the scenes helped each other. Also talk about the way the teams cooperated to prepare the scenes.

Possible Scenes:

1. The group is going to play a game together and the captains are choosing sides. You are not chosen for either team. A classmate is walking toward you,

and you feel like running to hide.

2. Your best friend has just told you that he is moving away from town. You have been best friends for a long time, and you are feeling quite upset. Another friend you don't know too well is coming over to talk with you.

3. You have just fallen down and skinned your legs. Your books have skidded all over the sidewalk, and you are embarrassed. A man is walking toward you.

Working Together In The World

Give the group ongoing experiences in cooperation and experiment in trying out new roles by providing time and props for individual and small group experience.

Provide ideas and properties for group members to try a variety of roles which may be new to them. Allow them to work singly or in small groups to "be" a variety of persons involved in a variety of socially cooperative experiences. Collect or invite their help in collecting as many kinds of props as possible. Encourage them to "try on for size" as many roles as they like. This center can be maintained and increased over a period of time as space and interest indicate.

Encourage the use of chairs, cardboard cartons, card table with blanket covers, and any other available materials. Enlarge the scope of the center by encouraging decoration of "buildings" and "word-places" if appropriate.

Here are some ideas for possible role plays and props to support them:

Health Service Persons: lab technician, ambulance driver, nurse, doctor, medical secretary

Tongue depressors, makeshift stethoscope, bottles, cotton balls, uniforms, etc.

Postal Service

Badges, bag, "letters", uniform, hat

Food Service Worker

Uniform, coffeepot, salt & pepper, trays, etc.

Retail Merchant or Clerk

Simulated money and/or credit cards,

punchers, paper or plastic bags, "merchandise" boxes, etc.

Cosmetologist and Hair Stylists

Brushes, combs, makeup, wigs, cotton balls, scarves, aprons, etc.

Secretary and Word Processor

Simulated typewriter, calculator, telephone, writing equipment

Computer Technician

Pocket calculator, simulated computer

Farmer or Landscape Architect

Shovel, rake, seeds, bookkeeping materials

Mechanic

Pliers, wrenches, wires, etc.

Law Enforcement Officer

Hat, badge, notebook and pencil

Interior or Exterior Decorator

Paint brushes, swatches of cloth, bucket, wallpaper books or samples

The above are but a small sample of the possibilities which can be developed for the career-role center. Avoid old stereotypes of either male-female roles or worker responsibilities and "tools-of-the-trade". Engage the participants in keeping materials and role models updated. Discuss the cooperative aspects of various careers; model cooperation as a group.

ARTS AND CRAFTS

Group Mural

Make a community mural on a chosen theme by having all group members work together on a large piece of paper (newsprint works well). One variation is to have group members draw and color animals, people, buildings, trees, etc. separately and cut them out and glue them onto the mural. Before beginning, discuss the different ways people can cooperate and help in such a venture; after completing the project, attention can again be drawn to methods of cooperation that were used.

Collage Co-Op

Materials: Glue
               Scissors
               Picture materials

Invite the participants to divide themselves into dyads or tryads as appropriate to the group. Provide a variety of magazines and other sources of pictures and print including catalogues, discarded textbooks, etc. Invite each small group to hunt for pictures and/or words which suggest different forms of cooperation. Invite them to cut these out and design together a group collage depicting cooperation. When collages are completed, invite each group to share their collage, telling about what they have pictured and also to describe their cooperation experience in preparing the collage.

Cooperation Bulletin Board

Invite the group to note during its meeting times the activities which have been carried out cooperatively. Allow time at the end of each day of meeting time for these to be recorded either in picture or words. Post the verbal or pictorial representations on a bulletin board. Both individual and group accomplishments can be used. The progress and growth of the group will thus be informally charted. Encourage a variety of forms of recognition including words, symbols, objects, pictures, etc. The bulletin board itself then becomes a cooperative project.

Creative Cooperation

Materials: Sizable boxes
               Markers
               Tape
               (Newspaper, tempera paint and
                  brushes if desired)

Divide the group into pairs or small groups. Give each team a large box (appliance stores often have large TV or refrigerator boxes) and instruct them to cooperate on choosing a project and carrying it out by making their box into whatever they desire. Some possible projects are box houses or box furniture (stoves, chairs, tables, etc.). Watch the teams work together. After a suitable period of time, call them back together and discuss helping and cooperation.

Ideas for discussion are:

1. What parts of the project were easiest to do?

2. Which parts were more difficult?

3. What kinds of actions promoted the project?

4. How would you cooperate to carry out the project if you were starting it over again?

Paper Cooperation: An Exercise In Weaving

Materials: Colored or white paper of
                  desired frame size
               Glue or paste
               Scissors

Invite each participant to select paper, scissors and glue. Model the process of making a frame from a full-sized sheet of paper by cutting parallel slits, keeping a border of at least one-half inch all around the sheet. The cuts may be approximately one-half inch or more apart extending from top to bottom of the paper, but maintaining the border. Cut strips of varied-color paper the length of the frame and demonstrate how to weave it in and out through the slits, securing both ends to the border with glue, paste, or staples.

Invite the participants to design and weave their own creations, giving reinforcement, encouragement, and coaching as needed.

Give each individual time to talk about his project and his experience in completing it.

Use the entire experience to discuss cooperation as a strength-building quality. Note that the paper is strengthened as each strip is woven in among others in a cooperative pattern. Note that its beauty is enhanced as it becomes a part of a cooperating whole. Transfer this concept to group cooperation and helping.

Toothpick Sculptures

Materials: Quick drying glue such as
                  household cement or
                  Elmer's glue
               Toothpicks
               Cardboard or wood for base

Let participants form small teams which will cooperate in gluing toothpicks together to form three dimensional structures. Toothpicks can be colored with food coloring to increase the visual interest of the design.

Discuss the structures and the experience in cooperation and helping.

Cooperating Paper People

Have each group member accordion-fold a piece of paper, and draw a person on one folded section. Instruct him to place the center of the figure on one fold and the hand on the other fold. He can then cut out around the form, but must not cut around the hand. Large, straight feet will support the paper people. Tape the hand on one end to the hand on the other end and the result will be a complete circle of people holding hands.

Shoescraper Creations

Materials: Hammers
              Nails
              200-300 bottle caps
              Board or boards approximately
                16" x 20" x 5/8"

Invite the group to cooperate in collecting bottle caps and bringing them to the meetings. When a large enough number has been collected, assemble the other materials for a group shoescraper. Show how the bottle caps can be nailed to the wood, flat side down, to provide a scraper surface. A design may be formed, or caps may be nailed in rows or at random. Encourage group cooperation in making it possible for all mem-

bers to pound bottle caps to the board. Lead the group in discussing the various forms of cooperation which were utilized in carrying out the project. If possible, place the group shoescraper where it can be used by the participants.

Variation: Provide for individuals to make smaller scrapers which they can take home and introduce as a family cooperation project.

Cooperation Mural

Materials: Large sheet of butcher paper or
                newsprint as long as wall
                space will permit
              Many colors of
                construction paper
              Glue or paste

Draw or invite a participant to draw a basic mural picture outline for the project. The picture may be primitive in nature, a design, or any simple representation, but must have open spaces to be filled in with color.

Invite the participants to tear the construction paper into approximately one-half to one inch different shaped pieces and glue them onto the open spaces to provide color in a mosaic fashion. Overlap one torn piece on another and fill in the open spaces with appropriate colors. The design will come to life in a beautiful mosaic pattern which will be the result of group cooperation and helping. Discuss the experience together and decide whether the group would like to do this exercise another time at a later date. Use problem-solving steps to make the decisions, plan, and implement.

Cooperation Spinners

Materials: String
              Cardboard
              Large needle
              Scissors
              Decorating materials
                (crayons, paint, markers)
              Compass

Invite the participants to follow these instructions (model as needed):

1. Draw a circle on cardboard using a compass. Size may vary; experiment for different effects. Two to three inch diameter is average.

2. Cut the circle out of the cardboard and decorate it on both sides as individually desired. The edges can be cut in designs if they are cut equally all around so that the circular shape is maintained.

3. Punch two holes in the center with the needle. Let them be about one fourth inch apart.

4. String a piece of string about five feet in length through both holes, and tie the ends together.

5. Place the spinner in the center and pull at each end to spin.

Try cooperative spinning by having one person hold each end of the string and pull in "unison".

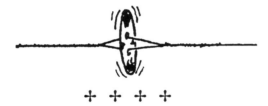

+ + + +

Cooperation Bouquet

Materials: Pipecleaners, variety of colors
Fabric, variety of colors
  and patterns
Scissors
Glue
Paper and pencils
Green floral tape

Invite the participants to:

1. Draw a simple pattern for the petals (see picture) and cut it out of paper.

2. Trace around the pattern onto the fabric; cut out six petals, leaving extra fabric (at least one half inch) around the tracing.

3. Select matching colored pipecleaners and fasten with glue around the tracing on the fabric, leaving one long end which will make up a part of the flower stem. Allow to dry.

4. When dry, trim off excess fabric so that the pipe-

cleaner outlines the edge of the petal.

5. Make a center for the flower by cutting a circle of material, wrapping it around a small amount of cotton or fabric. Extend the material so that a pipecleaner can be wrapped around it to secure the center during the assembling of the petals.

6. Combine the petals into a complete flower, assembled around the center with one pipecleaner serving to twist around the others and the center to hold the combination together.

7. Wrap with floral tape around all the pipecleaners and center to complete the flower.

Each participant may join his flower with the others for a cooperative bouquet if each is willing or use the actual assembling of the petals and centers as a cooperating project. Make sure that each participant chooses his own materials and is free to do as he wishes with his flower.

INDIVIDUAL CENTERS

Paint Center

Model helpfulness and cooperation by having paper, paints, brushes and an old shirt available for individual use when a person wants to create a picture, design, or just "paint". An old linoleum sheet or galvanized metal sheet is a good work surface. Press the paper onto the surface. Model encouragement and acceptance.

+ + + +

Science Center

Model helpfulness and cooperation by providing instructions and materials for easy, safe, science experiments. Examples can be found in science experiment books in the library, and can be as simple as growing a crystal garden, picking up paper with static electricity on a comb, shining a penny with vinegar, or rubbing balloons on wool or nylon and then picking up small pieces of paper with the static electricity. Model encouragement and acceptance.

✝ ✝ ✝ ✝

Puppet Center

Provide puppets and a simple stage. Participants can make up and enact stories which portray behavioral goals or for pure fun.

✝ ✝ ✝ ✝

Mind Teasers Center

Provide books with mind teasers or word puzzles in them, and provide a center with paper and pencils where ambitious individuals can solve the problems.

✝ ✝ ✝ ✝

Filmstrip Center

Supply a filmstrip projector, a blank wall or screen, and filmstrips. Explain the machine to the person, and let him show and view the filmstrips of his choice. More than one person can view at once. Rotate the available filmstrips often.

✝ ✝ ✝ ✝

"Things-To-Make-It-With-Art" Box

Invite all participants to cooperate by contributing simple household items and interesting "junk" to stock a box or boxes from which do-it-yourself creations can be fashioned by individuals or small groups. Provide shears (Pinking shears are especially fun), a stapler, paper punch, assortment of yarns, colored and white paper, pencils with erasers, crayons, glue, tape, and scissors.

Other objects with artistic possibilities are:

aluminum foil	cellophane
glitter	empty spools
pipe cleaners	gummed stars or seals
ruler	parts of jewelry
bottle caps	plastic containers
buttons	plastic meat cartons
sequins	wire
pieces of fabric	ribbon
lace	lids
feathers	assorted magazines
	for pictures

Most households discard many things which would take on a new, fresh value if found in the "Things-To-Make-It-With-Art" box. Model by enjoying the making of some free-wheeling creations. Encourage the participants to use their imaginations in "doing" what looks good and is fulfilling for them rather than working towards some final "product". Many have not had opportunity to create and have little self-motivation. For this reason, modeling, encouragement, and positive reinforcement are useful. Be sure that only those items which are no longer wanted are put into the box and give the participant freedom to work as he chooses. If several participants are creating during the same time period, a positive opportunity for helping and cooperation is available.

BOOKS

Picture Books

Beshow, Elsa Maartman, **Pelle's New Suit.**
Burton, Virginia Lee, **Katy And The Big Snow.**
Charlip, Remy and Burton Supree, **Harlequin And The Gift Of Many Colors.**
Delaney, Ned, **Bert And Barney.**
Delton, Judy, **Two Good Friends.**
Delton, Judy and Elaine Knox-Wagner, **The Best Mom In The World.**
Henroid, Lorraine, **Grandma's Wheelchair.**
Moncure, Jane Belk, **Kindness.**
Ruffins, Reynold, **My Brother Never Feeds The Cat.**
Thomas, Karen, **The Good Thing—the Bad Thing.**
Zolotow, Charlotte Shapior, **My Friend John.**

Fiction Books

Green, Phyllis, **Gloomy Louie.**
Hoban, Lillian Aberman, **Arthur's Funny Money.**
Matthews, Ellen, **The Trouble With Leslie.**
Morton, Jane, **I Am Rubber, You Are Glue.**
Pfeffer, Susan Beth, **Awful Evelina.**
Quigley, Lillian Fox, **The Blind Men And The Elephant.**
Reuter, Margaret, **You Can Depend On Me.**

CHAPTER 10

General Activities And Warm-Ups

GROUP PHYSICAL WARM-UPS

Find A Harbor

Invite the participants to form a circle with hands clasped, facing toward the center. Ask two members to remain outside the circle and be the "Ship Searching for Harbor". They are to clasp hands and roam around the circle looking for "harbor". When they decide on a port-of-call, they attempt to break the hand clasp of the that part of the circle. If successful, they take off running once more around the circle in an attempt to get back to the break which is now "harbor". If they get around and back before the two whose handclasp has been broken (who are meanwhile running in the opposite direction to get back) they have made harbor and a new "Ship Searching for Harbor" is outside (the two whose handclasp was broken). The game is repeated as long as desired.

Unravel

Invite the participants to form a line, clasping hands with the person on either side. The first in line is the leader. She begins movement by weaving back and forth, in and out, over and under the others in the line, always being followed by those behind her until she finally clasps the hand of the person on the other end.

A horrendous, tangled mass of persons will result. The object of the game is for those involved to untangle themselves and unravel the snarls until they are a circle. This is to be done without unclasping hands. One person may be named "Engineer" or "Traffic Cop" to facilitate the process.

Doctor, Doctor

Ask one player to be the doctor. She must leave and not peek for a few minutes. While the doctor is away, have the rest of the group join hands in a circle and get tangled up by maneuvering over arms, ducking under hands, or whatever they can think of to get themselves into a tight knot. The doctor must come out and untangle the group without having anyone let go of hands.[1]

Capture The Flying Tail

In an open place with ample space, invite eight to ten participants to line up one behind the other with each clasping arms around the waist of the person directly in front of her. The last person in line is the "tail bearer" and has a bandana or handkerchief tucked in her belt or back pocket.

The object of the game is for the front end to capture the tail from the hind end. When and if the head finally captures the flying tail, she dons the kerchief, clasps arms around the former "tail bearer" and becomes the new tail. The former second from the front becomes the head who now chases the new tail.

More than one group can be functioning at the same time.

The Human Machine

Invite the participants to go to the center of the area and act out the repetitive motion and sound of a machine part. Others are then to add parts to the machine, one by one, until the entire group is involved. This is an icebreaker and also allows portrayal of individual ideas in a spirit of fun.

Variation: The exercise may also be adapted to act out the participants' ideas of a machine which would manufacture empathy, loyalty, cooperation, love, and other similar concepts.

Human Wheel

Invite the participants to lie on their stomachs side-by-side and packed closely together. The person at the end of the line rolls over onto her neighbor and keeps rolling down the line of bodies. When she reaches the end, she lies on her stomach. Meanwhile, the next person at the other end has started rolling. The momentum of the human wheel will increase and surprise everyone.

Shoulder Slapping

Invite participant to form dyads. Ask one person in each dyad to slap her partner's arms from shoulders to fingertips. Ask her to move up and down the entire arm three times, doing an especially thorough job over the shoulders. Switch positions when finished so that both partners experience giving and receiving.

Head Lifts

Invite participants to form dyads. Person "A" will lie on her back, relaxing her head and neck. Person "B" will lift person "A's" head and rotate it. Practice relaxing shoulder and neck muscles while working as partners. Exchange positions so that partner "A" is holding and lifting, partner "B" is relaxing.

Outsider

Have the group form a circle by locking arms. Instruct one member to walk around the circle as the "outsider". She may ask for admission into the circle or try to force her way in. Take turns experiencing being outside and trying to get in. Share feelings about this activity.

Teletype Warm-Up

Designate four or five persons to be a "teletype" machine. Place them in a semi-circle. Add other "teletypes" as participants are willing. Insert a "card" into one of the teletypes by saying the first word of a sentence such as "Life...", "School...", "My family..." or "The world..." The teletype responds by constructing the remainder of the sentence, one word from each person. When one person says "period", "question mark", or "exclamation point", the sentence ends. Repeat with each of the teletypes. Invite the teletypes to ask questions of the other teletypes.

Trust Fall

Divide the group into pairs and ask one partner in each team to fall backwards into the arms of the other partner. Encourage her to hold legs straight and locked, and to depend on the partner to catch her. The closer the "faller" is to the "catcher", the less impact or sense of falling. The farther the "faller" is from the "catcher", the greater the sense of falling. This is a trust-builder.

Team Foot-Rubs

Have persons divide into pairs. One person can rub her partner's foot while the partner rubs her's. Encourage them to experience with different techniques of foot rubbing, and to give feedback about what feels good to their own feet.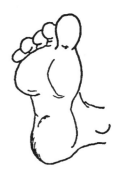

Trees And Clouds

Divide the group by twos and have one partner stand in an inner circle and the other partner in an outer circle, leaving enough space between to stretch arms.

The inside persons are the tress and the outside persons are the clouds. In this activity, the clouds will "minister to" the trees. The group can be divided by asking the people who are "up" to be the clouds, and the people who are "down" to be the trees (the leader can be a cloud if she is needed to make it even). Call the action, keeping your voice quiet but firm. Instruct the trees to tell their clouds that they trust the clouds to be good to them. Instruct the clouds to begin thinking good thoughts about their trees. The trees may close their eyes and let the clouds take care of them for the next few minutes.

Now tell them something like this: "Clouds, please lift your hands up over your trees' head and hold them, palms cupped around the head, about five inches from the head (demonstrate). Imagine your strength and love radiating from your hands downward to your tree through its body. Gently and slowly move your hands down until they rest lightly on the head of your tree. Hold them gently there and gradually begin to exert pressure and move your fingers in a quiet, soothing manner. Massage with gentle pressure as the rain falling upon the tree in springtime."

"As you are soothing away the cares and hurts of the day, gradually move your hands downward to the neck and shoulders, massaging and ministering to your tree. Now trees, you are invited to relax to a kneeling position and to lean back against your cloud for support. Clouds, please help your tree to a kneeling position and kneel as a support behind her. Now you will be able to continue your warm rain of massage. Sooth away the dust, dirt and cares of the day for your tree by using a 'raindrop' finger movement or a hand chop movement which starts slowly and quickens in pace like hail or hard rain." (Continue as appropriate.)

"Now, clouds, gently quiet your movements until your hands become still and have moved back to the top of the head. Hold your hands quietly there for a few moments, then gradually begin to lift them until they are about five inches away. Still hold them quietly and feel the energy and warmth radiating between your tree and your hands. Move them up and away like cymbals after they are sounded. Then bring them to your sides and quietly wait as your tree gets ready to once again speak to you."

When the trees are ready, they may feel free to turn to their partner and thank them for this experience. Be sure to have a sharing time after the activity.

Blind Touch Walk

Ask group members to walk around in a circle with closed eyes and recognize one another silently by touch without sound or sight. If anyone becomes uneasy or uncomfortable, she can open her eyes, sit down and watch for a few minutes until she is ready to resume her walk.

Reflections

Invite the participants to form dyads or partnerships and to stand silently facing each other. At the leader's signal, all are to freeze in their positions. Suggest that each individual take note of her own body position, how she is standing, her body posture, head, etc. Then have each participant ask herself: "How do I feel in this position? What does it express? Does it express what I feel and think about myself at this time?"

Invite each participant to take note of the physical stance of her partner. How is she standing? How is her head held? What does her body express? In this same frozen position, invite each participant to express to her partner things of which she is aware both in herself and in her partner. Each can check perceptions with the other.

Take time in the group to discuss what discoveries may have occurred through this activity. Encourage sharing and openness.

Making Weather

Form a circle with a leader in the center. Ask the leader to put the palms of her hands together in a praying posture and go around the circle, pointing palms together at one and then another of the group. This is the cue for the person pointed out to place her hands together in similar fashion. When all have been "pointed out", have the leader begin rubbing her palms together and pointing around the circle. As the pointed hands reach each person, they take the cue and begin rubbing their palms together also. This is the sound of wind. When all are activated, the leader then begins snapping fingers of both hands and persons in the circle pick up that cue and start snapping their fingers also. This is the sound of rain. The leader can go back and forth from palm rubbing to finger snapping as desired or make up other movements. No speaking is to occur. The process will be reversed from finger snapping to palm rubbing to quiet palms together to hands parted for a finish up.

Variation: Go from palms together to palms paired up with the neighbor on each side, right hand or left hand. The rain-making is then done in a chain so persons in the circle work with each other.

Human Roller Coaster

Form a human roller coaster by having persons make a single line with each person hanging onto the waist of the person in front of her. One person who is not in the line runs the roller coaster with an imaginary lever. This person indicates that the roller coaster is to go fast or slow by raising or lowering her arm, and the leader of the roller coaster follows the instructions. Voice sound effects may be added so that a low sound indicates slow movement and a high sound means faster. The human roller coaster sweeps around the room, with the leader responding to the speed control and leading the group at a walk or a run. Encourage the human roller coaster to stay together cooperatively and have fun.

Nature And Me

Invite members of the group to take a nature walk and to bring back something which best represents how they feel about themselves at that time. Discuss.

The Mirror Exercise

Invite group members to form dyads without speaking. Ask one member of the dyad to pretend she is looking into a mirror and the other member of the dyad to become the mirror. Instruct the first member to pretend such actions as getting dressed, washing, putting on makeup, and expressing various feelings as the second member mirrors the action. Discuss and share.

Live! From The Newspaper

Divide into groups of four or five. Give each group a newspaper and invite them to select one article which they will enact for the other groups as follows:

1. Set the scene for the event.

2. Introduce the characters, each character presenting herself.

3. Establish the time and place through fantasizing the scene in detail.

4. Tell the story through enactment.

5. Discuss and share.

On The Line

Spatially create a continuum line for the group. One end will represent warmth; the other cold. Ask all members to immediately place themselves on the continuum according to how they feel emotionally now.

Cold – – – – Warm

Variations: Ask them to place themselves on the warm, cold line according to:

1. Feelings for specific "known" people

2. Feelings about food

3. Feelings for specific events or situations (e.g. ball games, school, etc.)

Science Alive!

Invite participants to enact a scientific or physical phenomenon such as:

1. Portray a part of the body (arms, legs, heart, stomach, lungs, eyes) and explain its structure, what it does, and its relationship to other parts. Let each person speak as an anatomical part of the body.

2. Invite each member to embody a seed and to act

out the growth process.

3. Create visual organs linked to one another, and ask one member to be a drop of blood circulating through that system. Ask the drop of blood to speak and interact with the vital organs in order to establish their functions and relationships.

4. Enact the forming of the Grand Canyon. If desired, let some persons be droplets of water moving and interacting with the ground and earth.

✛ ✛ ✛ ✛

Rhythmic Rumbles

Invite group members to place themselves around the room next to an object or structure which will produce a sound if struck. Ask one person to start up a rhythm, and one at a time, other members to join in until everyone's rhythm is part of the orchestra. Share and discuss.

✛ ✛ ✛ ✛

In The Playpen

Establish the boundaries of a playpen large enough to accommodate the group members and allow them to interact as babies and toddlers inside the playpen. Establish rules of no slapping, biting, or hurting others. Allow the action to flow. Discuss and share.

GROUP VERBAL WARM-UPS

Remember That Name

Have each person go around the circle and introduce herself. Each person is to name those who have already given their names before she can introduce herself.

Variation: Ask each person to think of a word which describes herself and starts with the same letter as her name such as Silly Sarah or Jumpin' Jackie. Each person must say all the titles that have already been given before saying her own name.

✛ ✛ ✛ ✛

Get Acquainted

Have the entire group, leaders included, find a partner. Ask each pair to share names and a favorite

something such as color, sport, food, etc. (suit the interests of the group). Now, instruct each team to look for another team with which they can merge. When all teams have joined other teams, have each person say the names of all others in the foursomes and answer a question of values such as "What job can you see yourself doing" or "What would you donate money to if you had to give away $300"?

Now, ask each foursome to look for another foursome to join. Have them again say each person's name and go around the circle telling about one significant event in their lives, or some other question of personal growth. This activity illustrates that each group is made of individuals. It seems to help unify a group and give everybody "someone" with whom to relate.

✛ ✛ ✛ ✛

Birth Order

Invite participants to group themselves according to "oldest children in the family", "youngest", and "middles". Invite these subgroups to discuss their experiences related to birth-order positions.

Variation: Form "families" of oldest, middle, and youngest to discuss and compare experiences.

✛ ✛ ✛ ✛

Remember

Ask members of the group to think back to an earlier childhood time and to focus on a specific toy which has brought them pleasure. Have them describe the toy and their memories of it.

Variation: Have members be their favorite toy (role play). Discuss with the group.

✛ ✛ ✛ ✛

Drawing From The Well

Construct a "fantasy well" in full view of the participants. If you like, use various objects from the room or area designating what you see them as representing. Ask the participants to help in the construction of the well, then to individually approach the well and draw a bucket full of whatever they need. Inform the group that the well can give tangible items (e.g. warmth, esteem, love, money, car, food, etc.). After something has been drawn from the well, each member must specify how the item will be used.

Variation: Each member may demonstrate how the item drawn from the well is used. For instance, if respect is drawn from the well, the member might demonstrate giving respect to someone in the group.

Values

To break a group into subgroups for quick getting-to-know-you interactions, read off a set of three statements reflecting values of one kind of another. Each member decides which one of the statements she considers most important. The participants are then divided into smaller groups according to their choices.

For example, the items might be: "To be generous toward other people", "To be my own boss", and "To have understanding friends". All those who choose "To be generous toward other people" will gather in one subgroup to talk over their choices for a few minutes, etc.

Warm Fuzzies

Ask persons to give out warm fuzzies to everyone by sharing such statements as "I like it when you…", "I like it because you …", or "I like you because…" Make sure that all have a chance to receive and give.

Call Me…

Invite each group member to give the name she wishes to be called and share what she hopes to get from her experience with the group.

Variation: Ask each person to give her first name and a memory or feeling tied to her name. Let her choose a different name if she prefers it in the group.

Variation: Go around the group, each pronouncing her first name three different ways, then designating her preferred pronunciation.

Self Rehearsals

Ask persons to prepare their person self-rehearsals or affirmations for that particular time. Encourage them to make positive statements and to say them over at least three times, emphasizing a different word each time. For example, "*I* am going to be helpful this evening", "I *am* intelligent and prepared", or "I am *going* to do excellent work today". Go around the circle and share self-rehearsals.

Water Warm Up

Invite each participant to share with the group what form of water represents her state of mind at that particular time (e.g. a rushing stream, waves pounding on the ocean shore, an ice cube melting in the sun, etc.). Encourage sharing and open exchange.

Warm-Up Fun

Ask persons to sit in a circle and to share on a topic such as:

1. If you were a form of water, what would you be tonight? (stream, rain, waterfall, ice cube, etc.)

2. What is your personal classified ad for this moment? (help wanted, parents for rent, English tutor needed, etc.)

3. What is your own inner weather condition and weather forecast? (partly cloudy with a chance of rain, freezing, sunny, etc.)

4. What is one new or good thing that has happened to you today?

5. What is one significant event of your life which has influenced your growth as a person?

6. If you were an animal (plant, vegetable, etc.), what kind would you be and why?

7. If you could choose an ideal family, what would it be like?

8. If you were a color, which one would you be and why?

Inner-Outer Circle

Form two concentric circles with an equal number of people in each. Have the inner circle face the outer circle, and the outer circle face in so the persons are in pairs. For two minutes, have the pair discuss a topic. When the two minute signal is given, have the inner circle rotate clockwise one person, so new pairs are formed. Give a new discussion topic. Rotate until all members of the inner circle have talked with all members of the outer circle. Discuss the feelings and barriers involved in communication. Some possible questions are:

1. Ask each pair to tell each other about the first home they can remember as a child. Describe it in detail, telling as much about color, dimension, shape, smell and sounds as can be remembered.

2. Ask each pair to share by introducing each other to an important person in their lives when they were children. Describe that person in loving detail and share about the beliefs, actions, and impact of that individual on the sharer.

3. Ask each pair to tell each other about themselves as a child, describing, sharing feelings, beliefs, and whatever experiences they wish to tell their partners.

4. Ask each pair to tell each other about how they are different now from that child they have described.

5. Ask each pair to tell each other about how they would like to be in five years (or one year).

Parent's Chat

Have persons pair up and imagine that they are one of their own parents. They must decide which of their parents they will become, and imagine that they have met a parent of another child and are talking about their own child (in other words, you are talking about yourself as you imagine your parents might talk about you). Encourage them to talk about what their children have done with their lives, how they each feel about their child, how well the child has met their expectations, how the child compares with their other children, or whatever seems important.

Now take a few minutes to discuss what persons have discovered through this experience. How did they feel about pretending to be their parents? What did they notice about their partner's "parent" and what did they discover about themselves?[2]

Three Things About Me

Form groups of two or three. Let each person take a turn telling her name and three good things about herself. These three things can be divided into intellectual, physical, and emotional categories. The next group member must repeat back the previous person's name and the three things before telling about herself.

Mutual Interview

Invite the group to divide into teams of two. Give each dyad ten minutes for a two-way interview. Ask each person then to introduce her partner to the group, telling what she has learned about her. After introductions have been completed, discuss the kinds of information shared. Note what seemed important to share. Exchange individual hopes for knowing group members.

Sharing Activity

Ask persons to share with the group on personal topics such as:

1. An incident from their childhood that is important to them now.

2. The happiest moment in their lives.

3. The most embarrassing moment in their lives.

4. A personal secret.

5. Their feelings about a part of their bodies that they like the most, or that they like the least.

6. How they feel about their work or school.

7. Their feelings about other members of the group.

Design A T-Shirt

Based on how the person is feeling right now, have her design an imaginary T-shirt and tell what it says and how it looks including color.

Variation: Let persons actually draw out their T-shirt designs.

WHILE YOU WAIT GAMES

Bubble Gum Blowing Contest

Give prizes or verbal "I" message recognitions for the biggest bubble, the loudest bubble, the most creative bubble, the smallest bubble and anything else you can think of.

Simon Says

The leader (Simon) leads the group, but the group only cooperates when Simon starts with the words "Simon says..." However, a new dimension is added. Simon must also say "Simon says 'I want you to...'." or "Simon says 'I would like for you to'." If Simon leaves off either "Simon says" or the "I" message, the group is to reject his request. Vary leadership among the group.

Red Rover

Form two teams and have teams members join hands. The teams will face each other, standing about fifteen feet apart. The first team chants the challenge: Red Rover, we want you to send _____ over" and inserts the name of one of the opposing team members in the blank. That person then runs across to the other team and tries to break through the grasp of two team members. If successful, she can take back one of those who hands were opened. If unsuccessful, she must stay with the opposing team provided each of the two players where she tried to break through give her a positive "I" message such as "I want you to be on this team", "I think you're a good player" etc. Encourage positive, on-the-level messages. If a message seems phony, ask the giver "Is that a real message, _____?" If not, encourage and coach for a level, real "I" message.

Mother Or Father "May I"?

All players start at a line about ten feet back from the "Mother" or "Father", and attempt to reach her by requesting permission from her to take steps in her direction. They must being their requests with the words "Mother or Father, may I..." or their request will be refused. The first to reach the parent is the new "Mother" or "Father". When the "Mother" or "Father" gives permission, a positive "I" message is to be included such as "I like it when you..." Other possible starters are "I think you." and "(I) thank you for..."

Drop The Handkerchief

The group forms a circle facing in and one person ("it") skips around the circle with a handkerchief. She drops it behind someone who must grab it, run after the one who dropped it and attempt to tag her before she gets back to the opening in the circle. If she succeeds in tagging "it", she rejoins the circle and "it" repeats the process. If "it" reaches the opening in the circle without being tagged, "it" joins the circle and the other person becomes "it". The person who has joined the circle must give an "I" message, either positive or negative, before the game resumes.

Follow The Leader

All persons form a single file line behind the leader and repeat her actions. At the end of a set length of time, the leader goes to the end of the line, and the next person in line becomes the leader. Use learning concepts such as body language and portrayal of feelings as the basis for some of the actions. Reinforce and encourage.

Duck Duck Goose

The group forms a circle facing in and sits on the ground. The person who is "it" moves around the outside of the circle, touching each person's head and saying "duck". When she touches someone's head and says "goose", that person must jump up, and race after "it", trying to touch "it" before she makes it back to the opening in the circle. Whoever reaches the opening first is safe and the other person is "it".

Button, Button

Give each pair of persons one button. One person of the pair is "it" and will hold the button and both hands behind her back. When she brings her hands forward, the other person may guess which hand holds the button. If the guesser gets three out of five correct, she becomes "it".

Seek And Find

While the participants hide their eyes, hide a small object which has previously been shown to the group. Invite the group to look for it. Give cues with "I" messages such as "I think you'll have better luck looking higher" or "I put it under something wooden" or "I would look near something that makes light". The finder may become the hider and cue-giver.

Gossip

Sit in a circle and whisper a simple sentence to the person on your right. Have her repeat it to the person on her right and so on around the room. The last person in the circle speaks aloud what she heard. Great fun and distortion! Take turns starting the "gossip".

Rhyme It

Present words to the group which rhyme but have no meaning such as dop, frop, blop, and jop. Then give them robble, mobble, schnobble and sneep, dreep, fleep. Throw in a real word here and there along with the nonsense words. Invite participants to think of real or nonsense words which rhyme with common words such as hat, read, sad, or mop. Explain the difference between real words and nonsense words by definition. Encourage them to rhyme with both real and nonsense words but to differentiate between them.

What's It For? What's Missing?

Place five or six common useful objects such as a pencil, fork, plastic measuring cup, key, and scissors in a box or other container. Without showing everything to the group, invite one person to take out one thing at a time, letting the group give as many uses for each thing as they can in thirty seconds. Ask the group to close their eyes and let a participant take one thing out of the bag and put it where it cannot be seen. Invite another participant to look into the bag and guess what has been removed.

"Sounds For Guessing"

Invite the group to close their eyes. Make a sound which his familiar such as closing a door, striking a match, ringing a bell, stomping a foot, zipping up a zipper or pouring water. Ask them to identify the sound. Then give other persons opportunity to produce "sounds for guessing".

Variation: Use less familiar sounds such as tapping a glass with metal, dropping a book, or tapping a pencil. Improvise as desired.

Whispering

Use a paper towel tube or similar object, holding one end of the tube to the ear of your partner and the other end to your mouth. Whisper a single word, then let your partner try to whisper back the same word. Reverse and invite your partner to whisper a word for you. Can you whisper it back to her? Try whispering sounds such as SSSSSSH or EEEEEEE and have them returned. The whispering game is a fun way to learn to listen carefully and speak clearly.

Flippy Fingers

Invite participants to learn finger names as follows: "thumb, pointer, middle, ring, and pinky". The person who is "it" closes her fit tightly then flips up one of her fingers, returning it down again quickly. The group is to guess which one was flipped.

Variation: Make this a number game by flipping up one, two, three, four, or all five fingers with the group trying to remember how many were flipped. The game can also be played by drawing a symbol on each finger and letting the group remember which was which or which was flipped.

Charades

Act out books, movies, TV shows, famous persons, etc. in quick charades. Many variations are possible including team, individual, timing etc. Some like to play it with symbolic motions such as tapping the forearm to indicate how many syllables in a word, hands open to indicate a book title, rectangle to indicate TV show, or winding with one hand and circle hand formation with the other to indicate the movie.

Magical Ball

Form a small ball out of aluminum foil to be the "magical ball". Arrange three cups upside down and place the ball under one of them. Move the cups slowly around and in and out from each other. Let an individual guess which cup has the ball under it. If successful, she becomes the mover for the next "round".

Variation: Place several small objects out and invite the participants to close their eyes. Meanwhile, cover one of the objects with a cup. Ask volunteers to guess what was taken away and thereby become "it".

Penny Toss

Place two or three plates on the floor close together. Invite the participants to take turns tossing pennies into the plates. Count how many each is able to "land" into a plate. Then take turns tossing again. China plates are especially fun since the pennies make a "ping" sound and bounce a little.

You Message / I Message

The group lines up about fifteen feet behind a leader. The leader calls out "I Message" and turns her back to the group. This is the signal for the group to move toward the leader. The leader then yells "You Message" and turns around. If she catches anyone moving, that person is sent back to the line to start over. The first one to reach the leader becomes the new leader.

Finger Shapes

Hands and fingers can be used to form many shapes and letters. Show the group how to form a circle, square, triangle, cross, etc. Other shapes such as a tent, a church, or binoculars can also be formed. Letters can also be shown by using some dexterity. After demonstrating, call for a letter and see how many can form it. Give another participants leadership opportunity.

Variation: Invite participants to draw shapes with their hands or fingers in the air. The group is to guess what has been drawn. Invite participants to draw shapes with a finger on the back of a partner, taking turns drawing and guessing.

I Am Thinking Of...

Select something nearby and describe it to the other participants in the following manner: "I am thinking of something which... (has two legs, is in this room, is colored red, etc.). Keep adding clues until someone guesses correctly. Then it's her turn to select something and give clues.

Comic Show

Materials: Comic book or strip from paper
                  Scissors and tape

Furnish the participant with materials and invite her to cut out favorite comic strip characters and tape them to her fingers or to popsicle sticks. Now, she can put on her own Comic Show! Identify the names of the characters as she shows them.

✛ ✛ ✛ ✛

What Would Happen...

To play the short form of "What Would Happen...", give questions for the group to answer such as "What would happen if I took off my tie or scarf", or "What would happen if I unplugged this clock, sat on Joe's lap, went home two hours early, took off my belt?" Try out the answers if appropriate.

Variation: Use the game to explore feelings by giving questions like: "What would happen if Betty ate your sandwiches? If no one except parents could look at TV? etc."

✛ ✛ ✛ ✛

Footnotes

[1] 4-H Projects (Manhattan, Kansas: Kansas Cooperative Extension Service, 1978), p. 21.

[2] John O. Stevens, Awareness (Lafayette, California: Real People Press, 1971), p. 116.

Appendix

ACTIVITY RECORD LIST

Brazelton, Ambrose
  Clap, Snap, Tap (Educational Activity Records)
  Developing Motor Skills For Awareness (Educational
  Activity Records)
Disney, Walt
  Acting Out the ABC's
Disney, Walt
  Children's Riddle and Game Songs
  Finger Games (Educational Activity Records)
Good Apple
  The Ballad of Lucy Lum
Good Apple
  Dandelions Never Roar
Good Apple
  Imagination and Me
Jenkins, Ella
  Call and Response: Rhythmic Group Singing
Jenkins, Ella
  Counting Games and Rhymes for the Little Ones
Jenkins, Ella
  You'll Sing a Song and I'll Sing a Song
Merriam, Eve
  Catch a Little Rhyme
Palmer, Hap
  Creative Movement and Rhythmic Exploration
  (Educational Activity Records)
Palmer, Hap
  Feel of Music (Educational Activity Records)
Palmer, Hap
  Feelin' Free (Educational Activity Records)
Palmer, Hap
  Getting to Know Myself (Educational Activity Records)
Palmer, Hap
  Ideas, Thoughts and Feelings (Educational Activity
  Records)
Palmer, Hap
  Learning Basic Skills Through Music Volumes I-IV
  (Educational Activity Records)
Palmer, Hap
  Mod Marches
Palmer, Hap
  Movin'
Palmer, Hap
  Pretend
Palmer, Hap
  Sea Gulls
Seeger, Pete
  American Game and Activity Songs for Children
  Singing Action Games (Educational Activity Records)
  Singing Games (Educational Activity Records)
  Sound Effects: whistle, crowd laughter, heartbeat, birds,
gong, phone, and other sounds
  Walk Like Animals (Educational Activity Records)

FEELING WORD LIST

Love, Affection, Concern

Admired	Adorable	Affectionate	Agreeable
Altruistic	Admirable	Benevolent	Benign
Brotherly	Caring	Charitable	Comforting
Congenial	Conscientious	Considerate	Cooperative
Cordial	Courteous	Dedicated	Devoted
Empathetic	Fair	Faithful	Forgiving
Friendly	Generous	Genuine	Giving
Good	Helpful	Honest	Honorable
Hospitable	Humane	Interested	Just
Kind	Kindly	Lenient	Lovable
Loving	Mellow	Mild	Moral
Neighborly	Nice	Obliging	Open
Optimistic	Patient	Peaceful	Pleasant
Polite	Reasonable	Receptive	Reliable
Respectful	Sensitive	Sympathetic	Sweet
Tender	Thoughtful	Tolerant	Truthful
Trustworthy	Understanding	Unselfish	Warm

Elation, Joy

Amused	Blissful	Brilliant	Calm
Cheerful	Comical	Contented	Delighted
Ecstatic	Elated	Elevated	Enchanted
Enthusiastic	Exalted	Excellent	Excited
Fantastic	Fit	Gay	Glad
Glorious	Good	Grand	Grateful
Great	Happy	Humorous	Inspired
Jovial	Joyful	Jubilant	Magnificent
Majestic	Marvelous	Overjoyed	Pleased
Pleasant	Proud	Satisfied	Splendid
Superb	Terrific	Thrilled	Tremendous
Triumphant	Vivacious	Wonderful	

Potency

Able	Adequate	Assured	Authoritative
Bold	Brave	Capable	Competent
Confident	Courageous	Daring	Determined
Durable	Dynamic	Effective	Energetic
Fearless	Firm	Forceful	Gallant
Hardy	Healthy	Heroic	Important
Influential	Intense	Mighty	Powerful
Robust	Secure	Sharp	Skillful
Spirited	Stable	Stouthearted	Strong
Sure	Tough	Virile	

Depression

Abandoned	Alien	Alienated	Alone
Awful	Battered	Blue	Burned
Cheapened	Crushed	Debased	Defeated
Degraded	Dejected	Demolished	Depressed
Desolate	Despair	Despised	Despondent
Destroyed	Discarded	Discouraged	Dismal
Downcast	Downhearted	Downtrodden	Dreadful
Estranged	Excluded	Forlorn	Forsaken
Gloomy	Glum	Grim	Hated
Hopeless	Horrible	Humiliated	Hurt
Jilted	Kaput	Loathed	Lonely
Lonesome	Lousy	Low	Miserable
Mishandled	Mistreated	Moody	Mournful
Obsolete	Ostracized	Overlooked	Pathetic
Pitiful	Rebuked	Regretful	Rejected
Reprimanded	Rotten	Ruined	Run Down
Sad	Stranded	Tearful	Terrible
Unhappy	Unloved	Whipped	Worthless
Wrecked			

Distress

Afflicted	Anguished	Awkward	Baffled
Bewildered	Clumsy	Confused	Constrained
Disgusted	Disliked	Displeased	Dissatisfied
Distrustful	Disturbed	Doubtful	Foolish
Futile	Grief	Helpless	Hindered
Impaired	Impatient	Imprisoned	Lost
Nauseated	Offended	Pained	Perplexed
Puzzled	Ridiculous	Sickened	Silly
Skeptical	Speechless	Strained	Suspicious
Swamped	Tormented	Touchy	Ungainly
Unlucky	Unpopular	Unsatisfied	Unsure

Fear, Anxiety

Afraid	Agitated	Alarmed	Anxious
Apprehensive	Bashful	Desperate	Dread
Embarrassed	Fearful	Fidgety	Frightened
Hesitant	Horrified	Insecure	Intimidated
Jealous	Jittery	Jumpy	Nervous
On Edge	Overwhelmed	Panicky	Restless
Scared	Shaky	Shy	Strained
Tense	Terrified	Timid	Uncomfortable
Uneasy	Worrying		

Impotency, Inadequacy

Anemic	Broken	Cowardly	Crippled
Defective	Deficient	Demoralized	Disabled
Exhausted	Exposed	Fragile	Frail
Harmless	Helpless	Impotent	Inadequate
Incapable	Incompetent	Ineffective	Inept
Inferior	Insecure	Meek	Powerless
Puny	Shaken	Shakey	Sickly
Small	Strengthless	Trivial	Unable
Uncertain	Unfit	Unimportant	Unqualified

Unsound	Useless	Vulnerable	Weak

Anger, Hostility, Cruelty

Agitated	Aggravated	Aggressive	Angry
Annoyed	Arrogant	Belligerent	Biting
Blunt	Bullying	Callous	Combative
Contrary	Cool	Cranky	Cross
Cruel	Disagreeable	Enraged	Envious
Fierce	Furious	Hard	Harsh
Hateful	Hostile	Impatient	Inconsiderate
Insensitive	Intolerant	Irritated	Mad
Mean	Nasty	Obstinate	Outraged
Perturbed	Resentful	Rough	Rude
Savage	Severe	Spiteful	Vicious
Vindictive	Violent	Wrathful	

PUPPET CONSTRUCTION

Stocking Puppets

Take an old sock, put it on your hand, and you have a puppet. The toe serves as the puppet's mouth. You can glue or sew yarn for hair and buttons or cut-out paper for eyes. It can have paper ears. To make the puppet's mouth open and close, slit the toe. Sew a piece of cloth in to be the "inside" of the mouth. This will help you "talk" with your puppet.

✛ ✛ ✛ ✛

Puppets From Pockets

Check old pants or trousers; cut out the pockets. Then cut holes so that fingers can stick through. You now have a pocket puppet. Color or draw on the puppet to create facial features or glue paper cutouts, yarn, or cloth for hair, eyes, nose, etc.

✛ ✛ ✛ ✛

Finger And Hand Puppets

Draw a face on one of your fingers with a felt-tipped pen and turn it into a puppet. The puppet will be wearing a hat if a button or paper cutout is placed on the tip.

A hand can also be made into a puppet by drawing a face at the base of the first finger about at the knuckle. The space between thumb and first finger is the mouth. Make the puppet talk by moving your thumb up and down.

✛ ✛ ✛ ✛

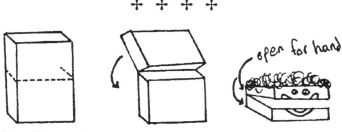

Box Puppets

Small boxes such as individual serving cereal boxes can be cut in the middle of the front side and down both sides to make a puppet. Leave the back all

in one piece. Fold the box in half. Add tongue, eyes, ears and a costume with paint, yarn, and other handy materials.

✛ ✛ ✛ ✛

Stuffed Puppets

Select some sticks, large twigs, or wooden popsicle sticks. Place a piece of cloth or a bag over the stick and stuff with cotton or crumpled newspaper. Tie the bag to the stick with string or a rubber band to form a head.

Paint the head or draw facial characteristics with markers, crayons, or glued-on shapes. Yarn, wood shavings, and buttons also make a good puppet decorations. A body can be made by stapling a little dress or suit to the stick. Scrap pieces of fabric or wall paper are inexpensive materials for puppet clothing.

✛ ✛ ✛ ✛

Glove Puppets

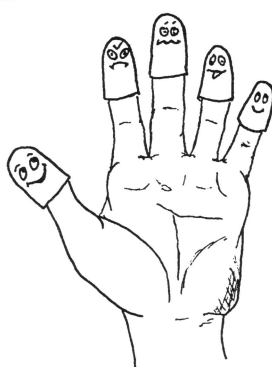

Use the fingers of old gloves to make puppet. With a pen or marker, make a face on each glove finger. Then cut off the fingers. The glove fingers, when placed on your fingers, become make-believe people. Make the glove people box and tell their names. If you want even more puppet people, make them for both hands.

✛ ✛ ✛ ✛

Bag Puppets

Use a lunch-bag size paper bag to make a good hand puppet. Paint or draw a face on the flat bottom of the bag. Make the upper lip of the mouth on the flat bottom part of the sack, the lower lip on the body of the sack. Insert hand into the bag and make puppet talk by moving the bottom (flap) up and down with fingers. Use yarn, construction paper, or whatever else is at hand to decorate the puppet. These are easy to do and work beautifully for a variety of puppet characters.

Puppet Theater

Find a carton with a bottom about 24 inches by 18 inches. Place the top flaps inside. Cut a section from the bottom to make the curtain opening. Leave an inch or so around the opening to serve as a frame. Tape some cloth to the sides of the opening which will serve as curtains. Paint the inside for stage and scenery. Place the puppet theater on a stand or table. From back of the box, move your puppets for a great show!

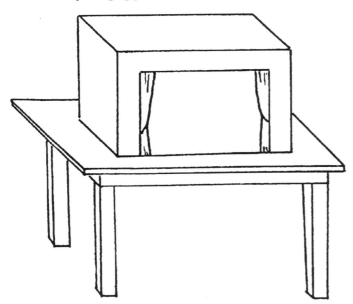

Variation: Make a "sheet stage" by securing an old sheet across a corner section of a room or doorway. Cut a rectangle 24" x 30" about 1 yard above the floor. This will serve as front stage for the big show!

RECIPES

Dough-Making Helpful Hints

1. Prepare large amounts of dough to give a good-sized piece to each participant to work with.

2. Mix several different colors of dough and invite the participants to knead combined portions which will make new colors.

3. Make cookie cutters, rolling pins, pie crust cutters, and other tools available, but encourage a high level of direct contact with the dough.

4. If liquid food coloring is to be used, add color to water *before* it is mixed with flour. If dry color is used, add it to the flour *before* adding water.

Making Dough

This recipe makes a grainy, elastic dough which can be baked into hard forms:

> 20 drops food color
> ½ cup water
> 1 cup flour
> ½ cup salt

Add food color to water and mix. Combine flour and salt until they are completely blended. Add colored water a little at a time, using enough to produce a soft, non-sticky dough. Take at least five minutes to knead the dough. If it tends to be sticky, add flour.

The dough should be soft so that it will work easily, but should not be sticky to the hands. It will keep well if placed in a covered jar or plastic bag in the refrigerator.

Variation: Mix 4 cups flour, 1 cup salt, and enough water (about 1½-2 cups) to produce a stiff dough. Dough will form easily into shapes so let persons make dough people, jewelry or other fun objects to bake and keep. Make other materials available to use in dough creations (e.g. rocks, peas, macaroni, beans, buttons and other scrap materials). Bake in a slow oven (about 250 degrees) for one hour. An antiqued effect an be gained by brushing on condensed milk before baking. A mixture of condensed milk and food coloring may be used for added effect. Paint the baked forms if desired.

Play Dough

Ingredients: 1 cup flour
                   ½ cup salt
                   2 tsp. cream of tarter
                   1 cup water
                   2 T. oil
                   1 T. food coloring

Combine the first three ingredients into a large cooking pan. Mix the rest of the ingredients and stir into dry ingredients. Cook over medium to high heat, stirring hard until a ball forms. Remove from heat and allow to cool. Knead ball until smooth. The resulting product may be used as play dough which can be shaped and allowed to harden or placed in airtight containers for reuse.

"Goop" For Modeling

Combine 2 cups of salt with ⅔ cup water and stir over low to medium heat 4-5 minutes. Set aside. Combine 1 cup cornstarch with ½ cup water and add to the warm mixture, stirring until smooth. Place the mixture over low heat and continue stirring. The "goop" will become thick. When cool, the goop will be suitable for modeling. It will not tend to crumble when dry as is the case with most clay products which are not fired. Beads, buttons, colored macaroni and other objects may be used in modeling. Store what is not used in plastic bags or an airtight can. This "goop" dries into a hard, smooth, white clay.

Finger-Painting Helpful Hints

1. Give ample elbow room and time for participants to do their finger-painting. This activity does not "hurry" well.

2. Finger-paint on a smooth surface. Dried paint will scrape off with a spatula.

3. Finger-painting can be done with cold cream or Crisco on a sheet of oil cloth. Use liquid food coloring.

4. Offer finger paint experience at different times during a day and in various areas (indoors and out).

5. Food coloring or powdered paint may be added to the mixture before using, or allow the person to choose the colors she wants sprinkled on top of the paint.

6. Invite participants to use warm finger paints and light, pastel shades.

7. Limit the number who will finger-paint at any one period of time.

8. Most any age group can enjoy finger-painting if an open, accepting atmosphere is encouraged.

9. Encourage the process rather than a particular finished "product".

Finger Paint Recipe

Combine 1 cup flour and 1 cup cold water. Add 3 cups boiling water and place over heat until mixture comes to a boil, stirring constantly. Add 1 tablespoon coloring as desired. Paintings made with this mixture dry flat and are acceptable without ironing.

Finger Etching

Take masking tape and apply to a smooth surface in the same size and shape as the "picture" is to be (newsprint will serve well to pick up the picture). Invite the participant to finger-paint on the taped-off surface. When the table-top design is finished, take it off by smoothing the newsprint over the wet design or picture.

Beads From Salt And Flour

Ingredients: 2 parts table salt
                   1 part flour
                   ¾ parts water

Combine the salt, flour and water into a dough-like substance. Add dry pigment or food coloring if desired. Pinch off small amounts and roll or form into bead shapes. Pierce each bead with a toothpick. Allow to dry thoroughly; then string them into a necklace or bracelet.

Translucent Paper Creations

Combine two parts of linseed oil with one part of turpentine. Apply this mixture to the back side of a drawing with brush or rag. This treatment will give an interesting translucent effect to the art.

✛ ✛ ✛ ✛⁓

Easy Pretzel Recipe

Preheat the oven to 425 degrees. Measure four cups of sifted flour into a large bowl. Sprinkle one package of dry yeast and a little salt into the flour. Mix warm water into the flour, working it with your hands until it forms a moist ball of dough. Cover and let rise in a warm place until you are ready to use it (not more than an hour). If you let it rise a shorter time, there will be less dough to form; the longer it rises, the more dough to use.

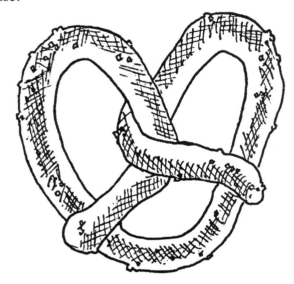

Give each participant at least one hand-sized piece of dough to roll into a rope and shape into people, "I'"s for I-messages, initials, symbols, hearts, reinforcement signs (R+), animals or absolutely any other shape that is encouraging or fun for the participant.

Beat an egg and apply it with a pastry brush onto the dough shapes. Sprinkle with salt and bake until toasty brown in a 425 degree oven for about 10-15 minutes.

Encourage discussion while the preparation is going on. When the pretzels are ready to eat, have a circle party and let everyone share "What my pretzel shape means to me and why".

P.S. It's fun to eat the pretzels with mustard and/or cream cheese.

✛ ✛ ✛ ✛

Another Pretzel Recipe

Ingredients:
 1 package dry yeast
 ½ cup warm water
 1 egg
 1 tsp. salt
 ¼ cup honey
 ¼ cup margarine
 1 cup milk
 5 cups flour

(course salt and mustard as desired)

1. Add one package of dry yeast to one-half cup of warm water in a large mixing bowl. Stir until the yeast dissolves.

2. Separate the egg white from the yolk and mix the egg yolk with ¼ cup of honey, ¼ cup margarine and 1 cup milk, adding this mixture to the water and yeast.

3. Mix in flour and salt enough to produce a stiff, but soft dough which handles easily.

4. Work the dough by kneading for about five minutes (use a floured board). Put it in a warm place and cover to rise. Let rise for about an hour, then give each participant a good-sized piece to work into her desired shape.

5. Shape the prospective pretzels into whatever suits the participant's fancy, and put them on a cookie sheet.

6. Beat the egg white till mixed with a tablespoon of water and brush over the "pretzels". Coarse salt can be sprinkled over the top.

7. Bake at 425 degrees until golden brown (15-20 minutes).

Index